ETHICS AND GOD'S LAW:
AN INTRODUCTION TO THEONOMY

WILLIAM O. EINWECHTER

Preston Speed Publications

A note about our name: Preston/Speed Publications
In an age where it has become fashionable to denigrate fathers, we have decided to honor ours. Preston is in loving memory of Preston Louis Schmitt. Speed is in honor of Lester Herbert Maynard. ("Speed" is a nickname that was earned for prowess in baseball).

Printed in the United States of America

First Printing 1995 Preston/Speed Publications

ISBN 1-887159-02-9

Preston/Speed Publications
RR#4 Box 705
Mill Hall, Pennsylvania 17751
(717) 726-7844

To the memory of my father

William P. Einwechter

June 17, 1918 - September 2, 1995

ACKNOWLEDGEMENTS

I want to express my gratitude to those who have helped to bring this work before the Christian public. Douglas and Beverly Schmitt have performed the invaluable service of formatting the book and seeing it through the publishing process. Their support, help, and expertise is deeply appreciated. I want to thank Rev. Jeff Ziegler for his encouragement and for his endorsement of the presentation of theonomy set forth in these pages. I also thank Rev. Andrew Sandlin for writing the foreword to the book. My parents, William and Dorothy Einwechter, are especially thanked for their support and assistance in bringing this book to completion.

A special thanks to my wife Linda, who, in addition to caring for our eight children, is a constant helper in my ministry. She also did the necessary and tedious work of proof-reading the book in its manuscript form.

The material in this book was first presented to the members of Covenant Christian Church, and then to those who attended the Symposium on God's Law and Socio-Political Reform on January 29, 1994. The feedback from these dear people, and especially from John Einwechter, John Fielding, and Joel Saint, have helped to sharpen my thinking and refine *Ethics and God's Law: An Introduction to Theonomy.*

Finally, I would express my gratitude to Dr. Greg Bahnsen who not only introduced me to theonomic ethics, but also convinced me of the correctness of this view through his book *By This Standard.* I have greatly profited from his other writings, and his influence on my thinking is evident throughout this book.

Soli Deo Gloria!

TABLE OF CONTENTS

A DECISION FOR THEONOMY

FOREWORD

The gratifying re-emergence of Reformed orthodoxy in the West after centuries of marked decline has been necessarily accompanied by a heightened interest in biblical law. This is not surprising, since of all expressions of orthodox Christianity none give greater emphasis to the relevance of God's inscripturated law than historic, confessional Calvinism. In his enlightening *Lectures In Systematic Theology* first published last century, Southern Calvinist luminary R. L. Dabney observed that "the view I have given of the Law, as the necessary and unchangeable expression of God's rectitude, shows that its authority over moral creatures is unavoidable." The orthodox Reformed have always maintained that the law is a reflection of God's immutable character and therefore can change no more than He can change.

In the present volume *Ethics and God's Law*, William Einwechter sets forth succinctly but potently the most consistent conception of this Reformed view of the law, today known as theonomy. The fact that this view has occasioned such controversy not only among modern evangelicalism (which is rife with antinomianism) but also the contemporary Reformed community exhibits one testimony to the extent to which the Protestant faith has deviated from its rich heritage.

It is hoped that Pastor Einwechter's clearly reasoned work will both buttress the faith of historic Calvinists in God's written law and convince others of the validity of this God-honoring view.

There will be no genuine revival apart from the dissemination of the pure gospel, and there will be no dissemination of the pure gospel apart from a revival of the Reformed understanding of the law.

Rev. Andrew Sandlin
Editor-in-Chief of the *Chalcedon Report*
and the *Journal of Christian Reconstruction*;
President of The National Reform Association;
Associate Editor of *Christianity and Society*.

INTRODUCTION

If there is one word that best describes the state of the world and the church in regards to the subject of ethics, it would have to be the word confusion. Now it is not hard to understand why the world can find no agreed upon ethical standard to deal with the moral chaos of the present age, but it is harder to explain the division in the church over the question of ethics. How can it be that the church of Jesus Christ has no unified biblical answer to the moral crisis of the hour? This failure ought to be deeply disturbing to every true child of God. This inability to give a well-articulated biblical solution to the moral morass confronting us dishonors God, leads to an unrighteous lifestyle among Christians, harms our neighbor, and hinders our witness to the world by contributing to the perceived notion that the church is irrelevant. It is sad to say, but it appears to be true, that "the salt of the earth" has lost its "savour" and it is now, largely, "good for nothing, but to be cast out, and to be trodden under foot of men" (Matt. 5:13).

However, there is reason to believe that this unacceptable situation is beginning to change. The Lord God, for the glory of His own name and for the advance of His kingdom, is at work in His church raising up believers who are fully committed in both principle and practice to the cardinal Reformation doctrine of *sola Scriptura* (only Scripture). By God's grace a growing number of Christians are responding to the ethical crisis in the world by applying the doctrine of *sola Scriptura* to the issue of ethics. This faithful and consistent application of Scripture alone to the issue of ethics has come to be known in our day as "theonomy."[1]

---

1. The name "theonomy" may be new, but the principle of theonomic ethics is not. Theonomy was the ethical system of the Reformed Church in Scotland, and of the English and New England Puritans. And it goes without saying, that theonomists contend that "theonomy" is as old as the Scriptures.

But, sadly, at the present time there is much misunderstanding in the church concerning theonomy. Some believe that theonomy is a dangerous conspiracy to destroy civil liberty and enslave citizens in the shackles of Mosaic law. Others see theonomy as a return to a kind of "pharisaical legalism" that tramples the freedom of the Christian into the dust. While others simply do not know what to think; to them the term "theonomy" sounds strange or even mystifying. What, then, is "theonomy"? The purpose of this book is to provide a basic and straightforward answer to that question. It is hoped that this brief introduction to theonomic ethics will give the reader a fundamental understanding of the essential aspects of theonomy, and also clear up many of the misconceptions about theonomy that are in circulation. Ultimately, it is our hope that the reader will be convinced that theonomy is the biblical approach to ethics and will be motivated to pursue further study on the issue.[2]

2.For further study of theonomy, please see the suggested reading list at the back of the book.

A DEFINITION OF THEONOMY

CHAPTER 1 - THEONOMY AND ETHICS

To understand theonomic ethics we must first define the words "theonomy" and "ethics." Having done this, we will be able to give a basic definition of the ethical system of theonomy.

The essential meaning of the word "theonomy" is quite plain. It comes from two Greek words, *theos*, meaning "God," and *nomos*, meaning "law." Therefore, our English word "theonomy" means "God's law," or, "the law of God" (cf. Rom. 7:22, 25; 8:7). So, even though the word "theonomy" may at first sound strange to us, there is nothing strange about its meaning; it simply means "the law of God" and is akin to the Old Testament phrase, "the law of the Lord" (Ps. 19:7). But to fully define the word theonomy, as it is used today, we must place it in its normal context. Theonomy is used as a title (label) to designate a particular approach to Christian ethics. Theonomy refers to the view that God's law is the standard for Christian ethics. Therefore, if we are to properly understand the meaning of "theonomy," we must also define the word "ethics."

Our English word "ethics" is derived from the Greek term (*ethikos*) for "morals." Morals are principles or standards of conduct that fix a difference between acceptable and unacceptable behavior. Therefore, ethics has to do with human conduct, and with the study of the standards of moral behavior. The goal of ethics is to establish that which is proper moral conduct by making a distinction between right and wrong. Ethics deals with "oughtness," i.e., it seeks to determine what a person ought to do among alternative courses of conduct. By establishing moral standards it enables a person to judge how they ought to act.

5

Noah Webster provides a helpful definition of ethics: "The doctrines of morality or social manners; the science of moral philosophy, which teaches men their duty and the reasons of it. A system of moral principles; a system of rules for regulating the actions and manners of men in society."[3]

Therefore, ethics, as a science, refers to the attempt to establish the fundamental moral principles which will serve as a rule to prescribe righteous and good conduct. The aim of ethics is to construct a coherent system of morality that teaches man what he ought to be, how he ought to act, and why he ought to act in the prescribed manner. Ethics seeks to answer three questions: "What is the motive of human action?"; What is the standard of human action?"; and "What is the end or purpose of human action?".[4]

Because ethics is concerned to put together a system of morality, the word is often used in reference to the code of conduct taught by a particular person, philosophy, or religion (e.g., Marxist ethics; Confucian ethics; Greek ethics; Hindu ethics, etc.). Hence, the expression "Christian ethics" would refer to the system of morality set forth in the Bible and taught by the followers of Jesus Christ.

What then is "theonomy"? Theonomy is that view of Christian ethics which believes that God's law as revealed in Scripture is the only proper rule and the only acceptable standard for judging the rightness or wrongness of any and all human behavior. God's law *alone* determines what man ought to do and why he ought to do it. Theonomic ethics, therefore, sets forth God's law as the supreme standard of truth and righteousness, and seeks to apply the precepts of God's holy law to every action of man

---

3.Noah Webster, *An American Dictionary of the English Language* (New York: S. Converse, 1828; Facsimile ed. by the Foundation for American Christian Education, 1967).

4.Cornelius Van Til, *Christian Theistic Ethics* (Phillipsburg: Presbyterian and Reformed Publishing Co., 1980), p. 3.

and to every sphere of life. Theonomy is simply the extension of the doctrine of *sola Scriptura* into the realm of ethics.[5]

Having given a basic definition of theonomy, it is necessary that we now go on to give a more in-depth description of the essential features of theonomy. This description, which is given in the following chapters, is crucial to a proper understanding of theonomic ethics.

5.Theonomy is often equated with Christian Reconstruction. It is true that all Reconstructionists adhere to theonomy, but it is also true that one could hold to theonomy without embracing all the theology of Christian Reconstruction. Theonomy is a view of ethics.

A DESCRIPTION OF
THEONOMY

CHAPTER 2 - THEONOMY AND THE SCOPE OF THE LAW

Theonomy affirms that God's revealed law is the standard for ethics. But what is meant by God's revealed law and what is the scope of this law?

When theonomy asserts that the standard of ethics is God's law, it refers to the *moral law revealed in Scripture.* The moral law is that law[6] which establishes the ethical standards of conduct for all men everywhere. It embodies the will of God for all men in terms of their character and behavior. Question 93 of the Westminster Larger Catechism asks, "What is the moral law?", and answers: "The moral law is the declaration of the will of God to mankind, directing and binding everyone to personal, perfect, and perpetual conformity and obedience thereunto, in the frame and disposition of the whole man, soul and body, and in performance of all those duties of holiness and righteousness which he oweth to God and man..."

The moral law is based on God's own holy nature (1 Pe. 1:15-16), and it establishes the righteousness of God that men are to emulate in their own lives (Matt. 5:48; Eph. 5:1). The Lord says to man, "For I am the Lord your God: ye shall therefore sanctify yourselves, and ye shall be holy; for I am holy" (Lev. 11:44). Since the moral law is a reflection of the holy nature of the sovereign God of creation, it must be universal (binding upon all men everywhere) and unchanging (binding upon all dispensations) because God Himself cannot change (Mal.

6.In distinction from the ceremonial law which dealt with redemption from sin and typified the person and work of Christ.

3:6; Jas. 1:17; Ps. 102:25-27), and as Creator He is King over all the earth (Gen. 1:1; Ps. 47:2). The moral law is therefore the one unchanging rule of right conduct for all men and for all time. It will be on the basis of this moral law that God will judge all peoples and nations (Ps. 9:7-8, 16-20; 96:10, 13; 98:2, 9; Acts 17:31; Rom. 2:5-12; 3:19).

The moral law is summarized in Scripture in the Ten Commandments (Ex. 20:1-17; Deut. 4:13; 5:6-21). The significance of the Ten Commandments is explained for us in the Westminster Larger Catechism:

> The Moral law is summarily comprehended in the ten commandments, which were delivered by the voice of God upon mount Sinai, and written by him in two tables of stone; and are recorded in the twentieth chapter of Exodus. The first four commandments containing our duty to God, and the other six our duty to man. (Q. 98)

But are the words of the Ten Commandments the extent of God's revealed moral law? Does God give a more detailed revelation of His will for man? And if He does, where?

In answering the above questions it is helpful to consider the meaning of the Old Testament word for law which is *torah*. Since we tend to define the concept of law in the narrow legal sense of explicit commands and statutes, an understanding of the Hebrew word *torah* is very useful for understanding the scope of the moral law. The Hebrew term *torah* essentially denotes the concepts of teaching, instruction, and giving direction. *Torah* provides men with instruction on how to live and reveals the principles of conduct that men ought to follow in their relations to one another and in their worship of God. Concerning the word *torah*, Jocz states: "The noun is derived from the Hebrew verb *yarah* (to throw, to shoot). In Biblical usage it covers a wide variety of meaning: to inform, instruct, guide, lead, etc. *Torah* exists to provide direction, to aim at the purpose of doing

God's will... it is never just law in the legal sense. It is wisdom, grace, an expression of devotion to God, a style of life."[7] It is through *torah* that "God shows his interest in all aspects of man's life which is to be lived under his direction and care. Law of God stands parallel to Word of the Lord to signify that law is the revelation of God's will (e.g., Isa. 1:10)."[8] *Torah* gives proper direction to man's life by revealing to man the moral conduct that God requires of him.

The law (*torah*) of God refers to all the moral instruction that God has revealed to man. Whenever God instructs man in his moral duties, there God gives His moral law. Consequently, the law of God is not only declared in the more formal law codes such as the Ten Commandments or the Book of the Covenant (Ex. 20:22-23:33), but God's law is also revealed in the context of historical narrative, prophecy, psalms, proverbs, and epistles! Therefore, the revelation of the moral law extends beyond the Ten Commandments and includes all the Word of God. The Ten Commandments summarize the essential principles of the moral law, but these principles are developed, explained, illustrated, and applied throughout the rest of Scripture.

Accordingly, theonomy teaches that the standard of ethics is the whole Word of God from Genesis to Revelation. The law of the Lord is revealed by Moses and the Prophets, and by Jesus and the Apostles. Theonomy is zealous to uphold the whole counsel of God (Acts 20:20, 27) as given in the Old Testament and the New Testament Scriptures as being the law of God. Theonomy avoids the error of limiting the base for ethical standards to only a portion of God's Word. Binding rules of conduct are found in all parts of Scripture. Theonomy affirms that *all* Scripture is given by inspiration of God and is profitable for

---

7. Jacob Jocz, "TORAH," in *Baker's Dictionary of Christian Ethics*, ed. Carl F. H. Henry (Grand Rapids: Baker Book House, 1973), p. 672.

8. John E. Hartley, "tôrâ," in *Theological Wordbook of the Old Testament*, ed. R. Laird Harris (Chicago: Moody Press, 1980), p. 404.

instruction in righteousness (2 Tim. 3:16).

Theonomy also asserts that the Word of God is a complete revelation of God's will for man, and as such, is sufficient to speak with binding authority to every issue of life. The law of God is perfect, and it provides instruction to equip us to determine what is right and wrong in any and every situation (Ps. 19:7-10; 119:99, 104, 128). We need no other source than inspired Scripture to define righteousness (2 Tim. 3:16-17). The Belgic Confession supplies a wonderful summary statement on the complete sufficiency of Scripture:

> We believe that this Holy Scripture contains the will of God completely and that everything one must believe to be saved is sufficiently taught in it. For since the entire manner of service which God requires of us is described in it at great length, no one—even an apostle or an angel from heaven, as Paul says— ought to teach other than what the Holy Scriptures have already taught us. For since it is forbidden to add to or subtract from the Word of God, this plainly demonstrates that the teaching is perfect and complete in all respects.[9]

The law of God sets the standard for personal, family, church, and societal ethics. According to Deut. 6:8-9, the law of God is to guide all our deliberations, all our actions, all that takes place in our homes, and all that transpires outside of our homes. The moral law is a comprehensive ethical blueprint which is to direct the individual, the parent, the elder, and the civil magistrate. All must bow to the law's authority and therein seek wisdom and guidance for every good work; for without the law and the testimony there will be no light in us (Isa. 8:20), but in the law of God we will find a true light for our path (Ps. 119:105,

---

9.*Ecumenical Creeds and Reformed Confessions* (Grand Rapids: CRC Publications, 1988), p. 82. The Belgic Confession was chiefly written by Guido de Brès who was a Pastor in the Reformed Church of the Netherlands. The date of the Confession is 1561.

130). We must never trust in our own wisdom in ethics, rather, in *all* our ways we ought to acknowledge the authority and perfection of God's law and allow it to direct our paths (Prov. 3:5-7).

Theonomy teaches that the law of God as revealed in the Old Testament and New Testament Scriptures is the sole authoritative standard of ethics, and that the Bible is entirely sufficient to instruct us in righteousness for every sphere of life. Theonomy's motto could well be *"the whole Bible for the whole of life."*

CHAPTER 3 - THEONOMY AND AUTONOMY

The ethic of theonomy is opposed by the ethic of autonomy. What is autonomy? The word "autonomy" is derived from two Greek words, *autos*, meaning "self," and *nomos*, meaning "law." Ethically speaking, autonomy means that man is a law unto himself. Autonomous man claims the right to govern himself according to the moral norms that *he* sees fit to establish; he claims the authority of his own independent reason to be the judge of what is true and false, good and evil.

So then, autonomy is clearly the opposite of theonomy; for as theonomy affirms the rule of God's law, autonomy affirms the rule of man's law. Autonomous ethics are anthropocentric (man-centered), while theonomic ethics are theocentric (God-centered). The essence of ethical autonomy is that of man establishing the moral norms of human character and conduct *by some other standard* than God's revealed law; whether that standard be human reason, tradition, religion, or philosophy. Theonomy is seeking to do that which is right in the eyes of the Lord (1 Ki. 15:5, 11; 22:43); autonomy is every man doing that "which is right in his own eyes" (Judg. 17:6; 21:25; Deut. 12:8). Theonomy is walking in the counsel of the Lord (Ps. 16:7; 32:8; 73:24); autonomy is walking in one's own counsel (Ps. 81:12) or in the counsel of the ungodly (Ps. 1:1). Perhaps one of the clearest statements in Scripture that contrasts the way of theonomy and the way of autonomy is found in Jer. 7:23-24:

> But this thing commanded I them, saying, Obey my voice, and I will be your God, and ye shall be my people: and walk ye in all the ways that I have commanded you, that it may be well unto

16

you. But they hearkened not, nor inclined their ear, but walked in the counsels and in the imagination of their evil heart, and went backward, and not forward (cf. also Jer. 10:2-3; 11:8; 18:12; 23:17).

Any ethical system that rejects the law of God as the sole and supreme standard of right and wrong, must necessarily be an ethical system which is at its core autonomous, i.e., a law unto itself. If God is the creator of all things, then His holy nature must be the standard of holiness and righteousness among men who are created in His image (Gen. 1:27; 1 Pe. 1:14-16; Col. 3:10; Eph. 4:24). God's revealed law, which is a transcript of His holy character, must of necessity be the only true rule that defines for man what is good and right, what man ought to do and be. Thus for man to reject God's law and establish some rival rule of ethics is to suppress the truth in unrighteousness and to worship and serve the creature rather than the Creator (Rom. 1:18-25). The promise of autonomy was central to the Serpent's temptation, "and ye shall be as gods, knowing good and evil" (Gen. 3:5). Satan's lure that led man into sin was the lie that man did not need to depend upon God and His Word for the knowledge of good and evil, but that he could be his own god[10] and know and determine these things for himself. Autonomy in ethics is man following Satan's lie and living out his rebellion against God and His law. It is man's attempt to be his own god. This autonomy in ethics is the very essence of humanism.

Therefore, there can be no such thing as ethical neutrality. Ethically speaking, there are only two possible options: theonomy

---

10. As Rushdoony has pointed out, "it must be recognized that in any culture *the source of law is the god of that society.*" Rousas John Rushdoony, *The Institutes of Biblical Law* (Phillipsburg: Presbyterian and Reformed Publishing Co., 1973), p. 4. Since autonomous man claims that his own reason and moral sense is the ultimate source of law, he is claiming that man himself is the true god.

or some form of autonomy. Either you serve the Creator and live by His revealed standards or you serve the creature and live by standards of your own making or choosing.[11] It is vain for a person to claim that they are occupying a middle ground between theonomy and autonomy, for that very claim is itself a rejection of God's authority and the rule of His law over those made in His image. *Scripture*, and *Scripture alone, must be the basis for our ethics!* No sphere of life has been granted autonomy by God. The individual, the family, the church, and the state (yes, the state also!) must submit to God and His law as the only true, infallible, and authoritative source for the knowledge of good and evil. No one has freedom to determine for themselves, or for others, what is good and evil. To claim such liberty is only to expose one's rebellion against God.

A deceitful form of autonomy exists in the Christian church today. This kind of autonomy gives lip service to God's law, but then goes about to determine which commands from the moral law will be kept. In this system, only those commands which are judged to be in tune with the times, which are considered workable for today, or which are in agreement with modern notions of love, fairness, and justice survive as standards of ethics. But for any man or church to sit in judgment of God's law, and to nullify or change any commands of God without direct scriptural authorization from God is autonomy, for in the end it is man's own wisdom and moral sense that becomes the standard. So many Christians today are like those in Israel who halted between two opinions. In one situation God's law is acceptable, but in another situation "Baal's law" (e.g., laws promulgated by a humanistic state, or by secular philosophers and psychologists) is found to be more in step with the times and much more work-

---

11.Biblically speaking, these are the only two options (cf. Matt. 6:24; 12:30; Ps. 1:1-6; Jos. 24:14-15)! As Christians, our starting point in ethics must be a full commitment to reject our own fallible reason as the standard, and to recognize the authority of God's infallible Word to interpret the moral sphere.

able and reasonable. But to such as these the Lord still speaks: "How long halt ye between two opinions? if the Lord be God, follow him: but if Baal, then follow him" (1 Ki. 18:21).

Theonomy is opposed to all forms of autonomy in ethics, and calls upon all men everywhere to repent of their rebellion and to embrace the law of God as the sole standard of ethics for every realm of life. Theonomists boldly apply the words of Jesus to the issue of morals and ethical standards: "no man can serve two masters" (Matt. 6:24). Autonomy is man serving himself and living according to his own law. Theonomy is man serving God and living according to God's law.

CHAPTER 4 - THEONOMY AND NATURAL LAW

"Natural law" is an elusive term today that means different things to different people. A secular view of natural law[12] will differ radically from a Christian view of natural law. And even among Christians there are differences of opinion on many of the issues relating to the definition and use of natural law. We must limit ourselves to a discussion of the biblical evidence.

According to the Bible, God reveals His glory, holy nature, and moral law through creation, providence, and man's conscience (Ps. 19:1-6; Acts 14:17; 17:23-31; Rom. 1:19-31; 2:14-15). We call this disclosure, "natural revelation," because it is truth shown to man through the works of God in the created

---

12.Henry gives a helpful explanation of the two major strands of thinking concerning natural law in Western philosophy: "Broadly speaking, two major traditions of natural law speculation have emerged. One conceives of natural law in a *physical* and *descriptive* sense. It represents an essentially materialistic and naturalistic tradition which seeks scientific explanation and attempts to develop concepts of obligation by appealing to the physical laws of nature. Utilitarianism, Marxism, Social Darwinism, and behaviorism are examples of modern attempts to construct ethical theory in this manner. The second major tradition of natural law speculation—which usually uses the term in distinction from 'laws of nature' or 'physical laws'—represents an essentially idealistic and rationalistic tradition which seeks normative explanation and attempts to develop concepts of obligation by appealing to teleological meaning and ordering within nature. In this sense, natural law is conceived of in a *metaphysical* and *prescriptive* sense. It seeks through the use of reason, to discover in human conduct absolute and universal principles of obligation which are believed to be lodged in the very nature of the human psyche and the universe." Paul B. Henry, "Natural Law," in *Baker's Dictionary of Christian Ethics,* p. 448.

realm. Natural law is a part of this natural revelation. Natural law is, therefore, the revelation of God's moral law through the means of creation, providence, and man's conscience. Because natural revelation is at all times and in all places clearly present before man and in man, all are accountable to it, and all will be judged by it (Rom. 1:19-31). Theonomy fully recognizes the biblical truth of natural revelation and natural law. However, theonomy also strongly affirms the insufficiency of natural law as the standard of ethics because of man's limitations as a creature, and because of his fall into sin.

Being a creature, man stands in need of the Word of the Creator to properly interpret and understand all things. God, not man, is the measure of all things and the source of all knowledge and truth, including the knowledge of good and evil. Therefore, even in the Garden of Eden when man was yet perfect and sinless, he needed the external Word of God to instruct him and guide him into the holy will of God (Gen. 1:28-29; 2:16-17). Man had an undefiled conscience, and creation had not yet been subjected to the curse, yet natural law was not enough. God's Word was required to teach man the path of duty and the way of righteousness.

If sinless man needed the Word of God and could not be guided solely by natural law, how much more must fallen man stand in need of the Word of God to teach him the knowledge of good and evil. If natural law was insufficient before the fall, it is doubly inadequate now because man's ability to discern natural law has been greatly affected by the fall. First of all, the creation itself is now under the curse of sin (Gen. 3:17-19; Rom. 8:19-22). Therefore, although creation still does witness of God's glory and power (Ps. 19:1-6; Rom. 1:19-20), it can no longer serve as an infallible revelation of ethical standards.[13] Secondly, man is now a sinful and rebellious creature who seeks to sup-

---

13. For example, the created world is now filled with violence and death. Should we conclude from this that violence and death are good?

press the truth of natural law in his unrighteousness (Rom. 1:18). It is certainly true that "the work of the law" has been "written in their hearts" (Rom. 2:14-15), but man's defiled conscience is absolutely not a trustworthy guide for discerning what is just, good, and right (Prov. 16:25; 1 Tim. 4:2; Titus 1:15; Heb. 9:14; 10:22). Can we trust the conscience of fallen man whose "heart is deceitful above all things, and desperately wicked" (Jer. 17:9) to be the final judge of what is good and evil?

The doctrine of total depravity teaches us that it is folly to believe that man in himself, or in counsel with others, will be able to establish a perfectly righteous ethical system on the basis of natural law. In regards to this, Van Til has said:

> This doctrine of the *total depravity* of man makes it plain that the moral consciousness of man as he is today cannot be the source of information about what is ideal good or about what is the standard of the good...It is this point particularly that makes it necessary for the Christian to maintain without any apology and without any concession that it is *Scripture, and Scripture alone,* in the light of which all moral questions must be answered. Scripture as an external revelation became necessary because of the sin of man. No man living can even put the moral problem as he ought to put it, or ask the moral questions as he ought to ask them, unless he does so in the light of Scripture. Man cannot of himself truly face the moral question, let alone answer it.[14]

The only result of making natural law the standard of ethics for fallen man will be confusion and error.[15]

What man needs is an objective written statement of the

---

14. Cornelius Van Til, *The Defense of the Faith* (Phillipsburg: Presbyterian and Reformed Publishing Co., 1955), p. 54.

15. If anyone doubts this fact, let him gather ten people at random and ask them to give their moral judgments on such issues as abortion, capital punishment, the redistribution of wealth, chastity, etc.

moral law of God. This is exactly what God has given to him in the pages of Holy Scripture. The Word of God sets before man the infallible standard of ethics. The Bible reveals the moral law with the precision of written communication. Man need not "search" for moral standards in the dimly lit region of natural law, but need only turn to the bright light of Scripture to read the explicit commandments and moral principles revealed therein (Ps. 119:105). The entrance of God's Word gives light and gives understanding to even the simple (Ps. 119:130).

This superiority of biblical revelation to natural revelation does not mean that there is any *contradiction* between the moral law as disclosed in nature and the moral law as stated in Scripture. The unity between natural law and biblical law is expressed in the London Baptist Confession of Faith:

> The same law that was first written in the heart of man continued to be a perfect rule of righteousness after the fall, and was delivered by God upon Mount Sinai, in ten commandments, and written in two tables, the four first containing our duty towards God, and the other six, our duty to man.[16]

There is only one moral law because there is only one true God who is the source of all things, including moral law.

Nevertheless, theonomy strongly asserts that biblical law is far superior to natural law as a disclosure of God's will because biblical law is written, infallible, objective, detailed, and comprehensive. Biblical law far exceeds natural law as a revelation of God's holy law. So then, we ought to "confess that both the *whole rule of right living*, and also instruction in faith,

---

16. The London Baptist Confession of Faith of 1689 is a Reformed statement of doctrine which is based on the Westminster Confession of Faith, and it mostly follows the exact wording of the Westminster Confession. Its main departures from the Westminster Confession are in such areas as baptism, and the nature of church government.

are *most fully delivered in the sacred Scriptures*, to which nothing can, without criminality, be added, from which nothing can be taken away."[17]

Would it be proper for man to set aside God's infallible written interpretation of the moral sphere and substitute this with the fallible interpretation of his own independent reason and fallen conscience? Certainly not! Therefore, biblical law should be recognized by all as the supreme standard of ethics. Let us affirm with David the complete perfection and desirableness of God's written law to even that of natural revelation:

> The law of the Lord is perfect, converting the soul: the testimony of the Lord is sure, making wise the simple. The statutes of the Lord are right, rejoicing the heart: the commandment of the Lord is pure, enlightening the eyes. The fear of the Lord is clean enduring forever: the judgments of the Lord are true and righteous altogether. More to be desired are they than gold, yea, than much fine gold: sweeter also than honey and the honeycomb. (Ps. 19:7-10)

17.John Calvin, *Brief Confession of Faith,* in *Selected Works of John Calvin,* 7 vols., ed. and trans. by Henry Beveridge (Grand Rapids: Baker Book House, reprint ed., 1983), 2:133. Emphasis added.

CHAPTER 5 - THEONOMY AND
ANTINOMIANISM

The word "antinomian" means "against the law" and, theo-
logically, has reference to those in the church who so stress Christian freedom from the condemnation of the law that they mini-
mize or even remove the responsibility of Christians to keep the
law now that they are justified. The cry of the antinomian is that
the Christian is "not under the law but under grace," implying
that God's grace in Christ has somehow nullified the believer's
obligation to keep the moral law. Antinomianism "is symptom-
atic of a pattern of thought current in many evangelical circles
that the idea of keeping the commandments of God is not conso-
nant with the liberty and spontaneity of the Christian man, that
keeping the law has its affinities with legalism and with the principle of works rather than with the principle of grace."[18] Hodge
states that antinomianism, "as the word imports, is the doctrine
that Christ has in such a sense fulfilled all the claims of the moral
law in behalf of all the elect, or of all believers, that they are
released from all obligations to fulfil its precepts as a standard
of character and action."[19] Therefore, the antinomian rejects the
law of God as the standard of Christian ethics.

Theonomy is squarely set against all forms of
antinomianism. Theonomy teaches that the law of God is the

18.John Murray, *Principles of Conduct* (Grand Rapids: William B. Eerdmans
Publishing Company, 1957), p. 182.

19.A. A. Hodge, *Outlines of Theology* (Edinburgh: The Banner of Truth
Trust, reprint ed., 1972), p. 404.

standard of holy living, and that all believers are fully obligated to walk according to the law's righteous commandments. Contrary to what the antinomian says, faith in Jesus Christ does not nullify the law for the Christian, rather, it establishes it (Rom. 3:31)! The Westminster Confession of Faith rightly says:

> The moral law doth for ever bind all, as well justified persons as others, to the obedience thereof; and that, not only in regard of the matter contained in it, but also in respect of the authority of God the Creator, who gave it. Neither doth Christ, in the Gospel, any way dissolve, but much strengthen this obligation.

This, however, does not suggest that theonomy minimizes the grace of God or the imputed righteousness of Christ in any way! Theonomy fully affirms justification by faith alone (Eph. 2:8-9), and glories in the cross of Christ (Gal. 6:14) and the grace of God (Gal. 2:21; Rom. 11:5-6; Eph. 1:6). Theonomy repudiates any attempt to base justification on the works of the law (Rom. 3:19-20; Gal. 3:10-13; Titus 3:5).

But those who adhere to theonomy also believe that justification and sanctification cannot be separated; for these are both part of the single work of God in saving His people from sin. In justification the believer is delivered from the *penalty* of sin, while in sanctification the believer is progressively delivered from the *power* of sin. And what is sin? "Sin is the transgression of the law" (1 Jn. 3:4). Therefore, sanctification must be seen as the process whereby believers are brought to increasing conformity to God's will by ceasing to be transgressors of the law and by becoming keepers of the law (Rom. 6:1-6; 7:25; 8:4; 1 Jn. 2:3-8; 3:4-9). Christians are to become holy as God is holy (1 Pe. 1:14-16), and to be renewed in the image of God's righteousness (Eph. 4:24; Col. 3:10). Where is the image of God's righteousness found? In the moral law which is a reflection of the holy nature of God, and in Jesus Christ who perfectly kept all the commands of the moral law! So then, the goal of sanctification is that believers be conformed to the image of Christ (Rom. 8:29) and glorify God by keeping all the commands of the moral law. The power for sanctification comes through the gift of the Holy Spirit who writes the law of God upon the hearts and minds of God's people (Rom. 8:1-4; Heb. 8:9-10).

The antinomian claim that grace releases a person from the responsibility to keep God's law is totally misguided. When Paul says, "ye are not under the law, but under grace" (Rom. 6:14), he cannot be teaching that the Christian is now freed from the obligation to keep the moral law, as the antinomians contend, for he has just said that believers must not yield their "members as instruments of unrighteousness unto sin" (Rom. 6:13). Since "all unrighteousness is sin" (1 Jn. 5:17) and "sin is the transgression of the law" (1 Jn. 3:4), Paul must be commanding believers to stop being transgressors of the law. Furthermore, Paul goes on to explain that Christians are now "the servants of righteousness" (Rom. 6:18-22). Since this righteousness is later identified by Paul as "the righteousness of the law" (Rom. 8:4), Paul must be teaching Christians that the way they serve God is by keeping His holy law.

Therefore, the phrase, "ye are not under the law, but under grace," *cannot* be teaching what the antinomians say it is teaching! Paul's point is simply this: those who are in Christ are able to break the dominion of sin in their lives because they are no longer limited to the resource of only a written code of commandments which tells them what they should do yet gives no ability to carry out those commands, but those who have the grace of God operating in their soul by the power of the risen Christ's Spirit are now able to obey the commandments of God. To be under law is to only have the resources of law. To be under grace is to have the resources of grace, i.e., the riches of Christ! Paul is very careful to make sure that his words about being under grace and not law are not understood in an antinomian sense by emphatically stating that he is not giving license to believers to transgress the law: "What then? shall we sin, because we are not under law, but under grace? God forbid" (Rom. 6:15). Grace does not teach the Christian to deny the law, rather it teaches him to keep the law (cf. Titus 2:11-12)!

The antinomian also asserts that his Christian liberty looses him from the responsibility of keeping the law of God. But this view is clearly unscriptural. True Christian liberty is not the freedom to set our own ethical standards in disregard of God's law (autonomy), but it is the freedom to serve God and live by the ethical standards of His holy law (theonomy). In Christ, we are set free from sin to become "the servants of righteousness" (Rom. 6:18). True spiritual liberty is to walk in obedience to God's commands: "I will walk at liberty: for I seek thy precepts" (Ps. 119:45). The law of God is "the perfect law of liberty" for the Christian (Jas. 1:25; 2:12).

A very prevalent form of antinomianism is the view that the Christian is entirely freed from the obligation to obey the Old Testament law because believers are now only under "the law of Christ" (1 Cor. 9:21). This view allows the Old Testament law to provide "wisdom" for the Christian in his ethical decisions, for the Old Testament is still recognized as inspired Scripture. Nevertheless, this wisdom from the Old Testament law is not considered *binding* upon the Christian, because these laws are *only* for Israel. The Christian may gain wisdom from the Old Testament law, but, apparently, he is under no obligation to obey it. These antinomians have thus created a new category of revelation: non-binding wisdom from God![20] This view allows man to sit in judgment of God's law, and to accept or reject its moral wisdom as *he* sees fit! This approach to Old Testament law greatly undermines Christian ethics because it nullifies one

---

20.I want to thank my brother, John Einwechter, for this insight.

of the primary sources of the moral law: the law revealed through Moses and the Prophets. In effect, this teaching cancels the *authority* of nearly four-fifths of Holy Scripture to establish *binding* ethical standards for today!

Theonomy strongly repudiates this antinomian view of the Old Testament law, and it does so for the following reasons. First of all, it is a very serious theological error to posit a difference between the "law of the Lord" (i.e., Yahweh or Jehovah) and the "law of Christ," because the "Lord" and "Christ" are one (Deut. 6:4; Jn. 1:1-4; 10:30; 14:8-11). There can be no fundamental difference between the law of the Old Testament and the law of Christ because there is only "one lawgiver" (Jas. 4:12; Isa. 33:22), and that "lawgiver" is Christ (Gen. 49:10)! The moral standards taught by Moses and *the* Prophet "like unto" Moses (i.e., Jesus Christ; cf. Deut. 18:15-18; Acts 3:22-23) are equally the Word of God and equally binding on men.

Secondly, Jesus Christ Himself emphatically taught the continuing authority of the moral precepts of the Old Testament law for His kingdom when He said:

> Think not that I am come to destroy the law, or the prophets: I am not come to destroy, but to fulfil. For verily I say unto you, Till heaven and earth pass, one jot or one tittle shall in no wise pass from the law, till all be fulfilled. Whosoever therefore shall break one of these least commandments, and shall teach men so, he shall be called the least in the kingdom of heaven: but whosoever shall do and teach them, the same shall be called great in the kingdom of heaven. (Matt. 5:17-19)

Jesus here declares that His disciples are responsible to do and teach the ethical and moral principles contained in the law and the prophets. As Calvin says, "we must not imagine that the coming of Christ has freed us from the authority of the law: for it is the eternal rule of a devout and holy life, and must, therefore, be as unchangeable, as the justice of God, which it embraced, is constant and uniform."[21] Christ taught His followers to keep the moral law revealed in the Old Testament. The "law of Christ" is that we love God and our neighbor by keeping the law of God (Matt. 22:36-40).

Thirdly, the Apostles of Christ also taught that the Old Testament moral law is binding for the New Testament dispensation (Rom. 3:31; 6:18; 7:12, 14, 16, 22, 25; 13:8-10; 15:4; Heb. 8:10; Jas. 2:8-12; 4:11; 1 Jn. 2:7; 5:2-3). There is not even the slightest hint that the Apostles considered the moral law revealed in the Old Testament to be abrogated for the Christian. To them, the law revealed through Moses was the "perfect law of liberty" (Jas. 1:25; 2:12). Paul summarized the apostolic view on the authority of the Old Testament moral law when he wrote that *all* Scripture (including the Old Testament law!) is profitable for instruction in righteousness for New Testament believers (2 Tim. 3:16). When God instructs us in the way of righteousness (i.e., gives us moral wisdom) He expects us to obey Him!

Fourthly, the express purpose of God in the New Covenant is to write His law upon the hearts and minds of believers in Jesus Christ (Heb. 8:9-10; 10:16), and to give them the Holy Spirit "that the righteousness of the law might be fulfilled in us, who walk not after the flesh, but after the Spirit" (Rom. 8:4). Now, what law is in view in these promises to New Covenant believers? It does not take a degree in theology to figure out that *it must be the same moral law revealed in the Old Covenant* (cf. Jer. 31:33); the law which is summarized in the Ten Commandments, applied in the Old Testament case laws, and expounded throughout the rest of Old Testament Scripture!

Theonomy repudiates the antinomian dislike of the law of God and confesses with the psalmist, "O how love I thy law! it

---

21. John Calvin, *Commentary on a Harmony of the Evangelists, Matthew, Mark, and Luke*, 3 vols., trans. William Pringle (Grand Rapids: Baker Book House, reprint ed., 1989), 1:277.

is my meditation all the day," and, "the law of thy mouth is better unto me than thousands of gold and silver" (Ps. 119:97, 72). The theonomist agrees with Paul, and believes that the law is holy, just, good, and spiritual (Rom. 7:12, 14), seeks to "serve the law of God" (Rom. 7:25), and declares, "I delight in the law of God" (Rom. 7:22)!

CHAPTER 6 - THEONOMY AND LEGALISM

It is important to understand that legalism is not to be simply equated with law or an emphasis on keeping the law. Legalism, biblically speaking, is not the use of the law but the *wrong* use of the law (i.e., a use not prèscribed by God). As with antinomianism, legalism has many facets and takes various forms. Let it clearly be known at the outset that the ethical system of theonomy condemns all types of legalism.

The most evident kind of legalism is the view that a person can be justified before God on the basis of their own obedience to the works of the law. This was the error of the Pharisees. It is also the error of Pelagianism. Equally false is the semi-Pelagian view that justification is a mixture of grace and works (e.g., Roman Catholicism). Theonomy strongly rejects any system of salvation by the works of the law. All men are sinners and transgress the law of God (Rom. 3:10, 23), and as such, the law cannot save them; it can only condemn them as transgressors who deserve the curse of the law (Rom. 3:19-20; Gal. 3:10). For sinful man, the law which was ordained to life (Rom. 7:10) becomes a ministration of condemnation and death (2 Cor. 3:7, 9). The only hope for transgressors of the law is salvation by grace through faith in the finished work of Jesus Christ (Gal. 2:16; 3:11-13, 21-22; Rom. 3:22-31).

Another facet of legalism is that of stressing obedience to the law while neglecting to also stress the spirit in which the law is to be kept. This legalistic attitude usually is caught up in a meticulous observance of minute details of the law (which one ought to do), but omits "the weightier matters of the law, judgment, mercy, and faith" (Matt. 23:23). The legalist fails to give true justice, to show mercy to others, and to love God from a heart of faith. This was another error of the Pharisees.

Theonomy totally repudiates such legalism, and teaches an approach to the law that, while stressing careful obedience to all the commands of God, does not fail to call men to serve God from the heart in the spirit of love and submission. True obedience to God involves *both* outward conformity and inward submission. We are to fear the Lord and love Him with all our heart, soul, and strength (Deut. 6:5). If we are to please God we must approach the law in the same way as the psalmist: "Give me understanding, and I shall keep thy law; yea, I shall observe it with my whole heart" (Ps. 119:34). An obedience to the law that is merely outward fails the test of true obedience (cf. Matt. 5:17-6:18; 23:13-33). Authentic obedience seeks the glory of God (1 Cor. 10:31), and is motivated by love for God (1 Jn. 5:2-3). Moses instructs the people of God in what the Lord desires from them:

> And now, Israel, what doth the Lord thy God require of thee, but to fear the Lord thy God, to walk in all his ways, and to love him, and to serve the Lord thy God with all thy heart and with all thy soul, to keep the commandments of the Lord, and his statutes, which I command thee this day for thy good? (Deut. 10:12-13; cf. Deut. 11:1, 13, 22)

Jesus said to His disciples, "If ye love me, keep my commandments" (Jn. 14:15, 21). The Lord Jesus also summarized man's duty in the moral law in terms of love for God and love for our neighbor (Matt. 22:36-40; cf. Deut. 6:5; Lev. 19:18). True obedience to the law of God begins in the heart and is motivated by love.

Another type of legalism is that which fails to emphasize or properly account for the centrality of the Holy Spirit in sanctification. In this view the law itself is given the power to sanctify; all one has to do is apply himself to the keeping of the law and he will become righteous in all his attitudes and actions. However, the law in and of itself, as a written code of commandments, does not have the the power to sanctify the believer. The law can command the way of righteousness, but it cannot supply the motivation or the power to man to walk in the way of righteousness (2 Cor. 3:6, 17-18; Rom. 7:6-25). It is the Holy Spirit alone who can enable the believer to fufill the holy requirements of the law (Rom. 8:2-4). God, through His Spirit, must work in us both to will and to do of His good pleasure (Phil. 2:13). The law is very important in our sanctification, but only as an instrument of the Holy Spirit to reprove us, correct us, and lead us in righteousness.

A final form of legalism to note is the practice of adding human traditions to the law of God. These traditions, which are supposedly based on God's law, set up human standards of righteousness, actually nullify God's standards, and lead men to transgress the true commands of God (Matt. 15:1-9). These commandments of men are used by the self-righteous to exalt themselves and to condemn all who do not live by their traditions. The Scribes and Pharisees used their traditions to condemn Jesus and His disciples! Theonomy has no place for such people or for their traditions! The ethic of theonomy is based on the commands of God only! Human traditions either add to or take away from the righteous standards of God's law, and all such tampering with the law of God is strictly forbidden (Deut. 4:2; 12:32).

Theonomy rejects all types of legalism and teaches that the law of God is not to be misused by men for their own justification or self-righteous exaltation. Theonomy holds that salvation is by grace through faith, and that the outworking of this gracious salvation means that believers will keep God's commandments by the Spirit's power out of love for God and for their neighbor. Theonomy opposes legalism by teaching that the motive of human action is love for others and not love for ourselves, and that the end or purpose of human action is the glory of God and not our own glory.

CHAPTER 7 - THEONOMY AND THE PROPER USE
OF THE LAW

Having spoken in the previous chapter of the misuse of God's law, it may prove helpful to establish in this chapter what theonomy professes concerning the proper use of the law. Paul said, "But we know that the law is good, if a man use it lawfully" (1 Tim. 1:8). We will briefly note six "lawful" uses of God's law.

First, the law of God informs men of God's holy nature and will, and of their duty to walk in obedience to God's commands (1 Pe. 1:16; Matt. 5:48; Ecc. 12:13). The law should be used to teach sound doctrine concerning God and man's responsibility to God.

Secondly, the law convicts men of their sin and just condemnation before God (Rom. 3:19-20; 7:7-11; 2 Cor. 3:9; Gal. 3:10; Jas. 2:8-13). The law must be used in the preaching of the gospel to sinners. The law works to powerfully convict and condemn the lost. Thirdly, the law functions to lead men to salvation by faith in Jesus Christ (Gal. 3:21-24; Rom. 7:24-25; 3:19-26). Having convicted men of their sin, and shut them up under the curse of God, the law is used to point them to their only hope: the grace of God in Jesus Christ! These first three uses of the law are stated in the answer to Question 95 of The Larger Catechism:

> The moral law is of use to all men, to inform them of the holy nature and will of God, and of their duty, binding them to walk accordingly; to convince them of their disability to keep it, and of the sinful pollution of their nature, hearts, and lives: to

humble them in the sense of their sin and misery, and thereby help them to a clearer sight of the need they have of Christ, and the perfection of his obedience.

Fourthly, the law is a means of grace for the sanctification of the believer. Through the moral law revealed in Scripture, God communicates His grace to His children (Acts 20:32). Jesus prayed to the Father, "Sanctify them through thy truth: Thy word is truth" (Jn. 17:17). A central part of that sanctifying truth is the law, for as the psalmist declared, "thy law is the truth" (Ps. 119:142). Furthermore, God resists the proud but gives grace to the humble (Prov. 3:34; Jas. 4:6). The law is a most excellent instrument to humble us! Fifthly, the law is the rule of life for the believer (Ps. 119:105, 133; Josh. 1:8). The law teaches the Christian God's will and restrains him from evil. The Westminster Confession contains an excellent statement on the use of the law in the Christian life:

> Although true believers be not under the law, as a covenant of works, to be thereby justified or condemned; yet it is of great use to them, as well as to others; in that, as a rule of life informing them of the will of God, and their duty, it directs and binds them to walk accordingly; discovering also the sinful pollutions of their natures, hearts, and lives; so as, examining themselves thereby, they may come to further conviction of, humiliation for, and hatred against sin, together with a clearer sight of the need they have of Christ, and the perfection of his obedience. It is likewise of use to the regenerate, to restrain their corruptions, in that it forbids sin: and the threatenings of it serve to show what even their sins deserve; and what afflictions, in this life, they may expect for them, although freed from the curse thereof threatened in the law. The promises of it, in like manner, show them God's approbation of obedience, and what blessings they may expect upon the performance thereof; though not as due to them by the law as a covenant of works. So as, a man's doing good, and refraining from evil, because the law encourageth to the one, and

37

deterreth from the other, is no evidence of his being under the law; and not under grace.

Finally, the law provides the basis for a just and well-ordered society (Deut. 4:6-8; Ps. 33:12; Prov. 14:34; Rom. 13:1-7). God's law, as revealed in Scripture, sets forth the perfect standards of civil justice. When the law of God is the basis for a nation's civil law, evil doers will be punished and further evil restrained (Deut. 17:12-13; 1 Tim. 1:8-10). The righteous will be protected and know true civil liberty (Jas. 1:25; Ps. 119:45). Christians will "lead a quiet and peaceable life in all godliness and honesty" (1 Tim. 2:2). The nation that honors the Lord and operates according to the standards of God's law will experience blessing, peace, and prosperity (Ps. 2:10-12; Deut. 28:1ff).

Theonomy advocates these "lawful" uses of the law, and rejects any use of the law not prescribed by God in His Word. The Belgic Confession states: "we still use the testimonies taken from the law and the prophets, both to confirm us in the doctrine of the gospel and to order our life in all honour, according to God's will and to His glory." The theonomist heartily agrees!

CHAPTER 8 - THEONOMY AND HERMENEUTICS

Hermeneutics refers to the science of interpretation; it deals with the proper principles of exegesis. In general, theonomy would hold to the historic Protestant principle of grammatical-historical interpretation. This indicates that theonomy calls for a careful exegesis of the Scripture which takes into account all the relevant data of any particular text. This data would include the syntactical and lexical details along with the literary, historical, and theological context.

The specific challenge for theonomy is to interpret and apply biblical law for our day and culture. This presentation of the theonomic approach to interpreting God's law will begin by noting three foundational perspectives which theonomy brings to this task. First of all, theonomy does not advocate (as some have charged) a direct simplistic transfer of biblical law to our day. Theonomy does not teach that one should take the laws given to Israel, and without a weighing of the theological or cultural factors unique to Israel, make these laws ours for today. Secondly, theonomy believes that the moral principle which informs (underlies) each command is universal and unchanging, and that this principle (once ascertained by careful exegesis) can and ought to be applied to our day and culture. In some cases it will be relatively easy to discover the moral postulate since the command is itself stated in terms of a universal principle; while in others it will be more difficult because the command is stated in terms of Israel's unique position as the Old Testament covenant nation. Thirdly, theonomy fully recognizes the difficulty of interpreting and applying biblical law. Theonomist do not claim to have all the answers or to have resolved every question on how to understand the biblical text. The job of interpreting and applying biblical law requires humility, diligence, and skill.

More specifically, the theonomic approach to the interpretation and application of biblical law is based on the following five hermeneutical principles. The first, and perhaps the most important, is the principle that only God the Lawgiver has the authority to add to or take away from that which He has commanded: "Ye shall not add unto the word which I command you, neither shall ye diminish ought from it, that ye may keep the commandments of the Lord your God which I command you" (Deut. 4:2; cf. Deut.12:32). Because of this principle we ought to assume the continuing validity and authority of each and every command of God in Scripture unless God Himself indicates in later Scripture[22] that a particular law has been changed, modified, or repealed. There must be a clear biblical warrant before we can say that a command of God is no longer binding for us today. It is pure presumption for man to set aside any of God's law without definite scriptural authorization to do so from the Lawgiver Himself.

Furthermore, since the moral law is universal and unchanging, we ought to assume a continuity between the moral requirements of the Old Testament law and the moral standards for the New Testament church.[23] Therefore, in terms of the Old Testament law, the Christian ought to consider its specific commandments binding unless the New Testament explicitly teaches otherwise. So then, the biblical approach to Old Testament law is based on an assumption of continuity, along with the recogni-

---

22. The progress of revelation and redemptive history leads to certain modifications in the law. As the plan of God in redemption finds fulfillment in Christ, and as men come to spiritual maturity in Him, there will be a corresponding development in the revelation and application of God's law.

23. A popular view in the church today teaches Christians to assume discontinuity, saying that only the Old Testament commands that are specifically repeated in the New Testament apply now. In other words, they believe that the Old Testament is really unnecessary as a source for ethics today. In this view, only the New Testament commands have binding authority for the Christian.

tion of the status of the New Testament as being the final authority on the use and application of the Old Testament law in this dispensation.

Another very important principle of interpretation is the recognition that Old Testament law consists of two kinds of laws: ceremonial laws and moral laws. This two-fold distinction is evident in many biblical texts: "To do justice and judgment is more acceptable to the Lord than sacrifice" (Prov. 21:3); "But go and learn what that meaneth, I will have mercy, and not sacrifice" (Matt. 9:13; cf. Hos. 6:6; Am. 5:15, 21-24; Ps. 40:6-8; 50:8ff; Jer. 7:22-23; Matt. 12:7). The *ceremonial laws* regulated Israel's worship, and provided means whereby sin could be atoned through the priesthood and animal sacrifices. Under the classification of ceremonial law we ought to include those laws which specifically related to Israel's separation from the heathen nations (e.g., the dietary laws, Deut. 14:3-21), and to their life in the land of Canaan (e.g., the inheritance laws, Num. 27:8-10; the Levirate marriage, Deut. 25:5-10; holy war against the Canaanites, Deut. 20:16-18).

The *moral laws* of the Old Testament defined the righteous standards of conduct for the covenant people of God. The moral laws are stated as general precepts and maxims (e.g., "thou shalt not steal"), or as case laws which prescribe conduct in a specific case so as to establish the moral duty for all such related cases (e.g., Ex. 23:4).[24] It is important to understand that the civil

---

24. The Ten Commandments summarize the moral law, while the case laws apply the moral law to specific situations. Rushdoony states: "the major portion of the law is *case law*, i.e., the illustration of the basic principles in terms of specific cases. These specific cases are often illustrations of the extent of the application of the law; that is, by citing a minimal type of case, the necessary jurisdictions of the law are revealed." *The Institutes of Biblical Law*, p. 11. Rushdoony further explains the importance of the case laws by showing their necessity. He says, "Without case law, God's law would soon be reduced to an extremely limited area of meaning;" it is only by analyzing the case laws that we can see how far-reaching is the meaning of the law. Ibid., p. 12. Also, the

laws of Israel do not constitute a third category of law; the civil laws are really a subset of the moral law. The civil law of Israel is the expression of the moral law in the terms of social and political ethics. Accordingly, the civil law of Israel establishes universal principles of civil justice and political righteousness.

It must be recognized that it is not always clear which category, ceremonial or moral, that certain Old Testament laws belong to. Nevertheless, these are the biblical categories, and we must adhere to them. A failure to properly discern whether an Old Testament law is ceremonial or moral will lead to the misuse of the Old Testament in this New Covenant era. Why? Hopefully, the next two principles will make this clear.

The third principle of theonomic interpretation is the New Testament teaching that the Old Testament ceremonial laws were typological in nature foreshadowing the person and work of the Lord Jesus Christ; consequently, the coming of Christ has brought about a change in the law and put an end to the observance of these Old Testament shadows (Col. 2:17; 1 Cor. 5:7; Heb. 9:9; 10:1; 1 Tim. 4:3-5; Eph. 2:14-15; Gal. 2:3; 5:2-6). The fulfillment of the ceremonial law in Christ, and the fact that these laws are no longer binding today is clearly taught in the New Testament. The London Baptist Confession gives a helpful summary of the ceremonial law and its relation to Christ:

> Besides this law, commonly called moral, God was pleased to give to the people of Israel ceremonial laws, containing several typical ordinances, partly of worship, prefiguring Christ, his graces, actions, sufferings, benefits; and partly holding forth divers instructions of moral duties, all which ceremonial laws being appointed only to the time of reformation, are, by Jesus Christ, the true Messiah and only law-giver, who was furnished with power from the Father for that end abrogated and taken away.

case laws must be of equal authority to the Ten Commandments because the summary cannot be of greater authority than that which it summarizes.

The coming of Christ and the establishment of the New Testament church has also altered the status of Old Testament Israel. Membership in the covenant people is no longer limited to national Israel, but is open to all who believe in Jesus Christ regardless of their national or ethnic background (Eph. 2:11-22; Gal. 3:16, 26-29). Circumcision and the identification of oneself with the nation of Israel has ceased to be a necessity for the New Testament believer (Gal. 2:3-5; 5:1-6; 6:15). The church of Christ is not limited to Palestine and the Jews, but is to expand into all the world and encompass all nations (Matt. 28:19-20; Ps. 2:6-9). Old Testament Israel was a type of the New Testament church, and the kingdom of Israel in Palestine foreshadowed the world-wide kingdom of the Messiah (Rom. 4:11-13; Gal. 6:16). Hence, it definitely follows that the Old Testament laws related to Israel's separation from the nations and to their life in the land of Canaan have also been abrogated since these were "typical ordinances" appointed only until "the time of reformation" in Christ and the establishment of the New Testament order in Him.

However, this does not mean that the ceremonial law has no value or application for believers today. As Calvin explains: "With respect to ceremonies, there is some appearance of a change having taken place; but it was only the use of them that was abolished, for their meaning was more fully confirmed. The coming of Christ has taken nothing away even from ceremonies, but on the contrary, confirms them by exhibiting the truth of shadows..."[25] So, when these laws are studied in the light of their fulfillment in Christ, they retain importance as a teaching tool to better understand Christ, His work, and His church.[26] The

---

25. Calvin, *Commentary on a Harmony of the Evangelists*, 1:277-278.

26. For example, Christians are released from the requirement to bring animal sacrifices, but the study of the Old Testament sacrificial system can help us to better understand the substitutionary death of Jesus Christ. Or, the specific

theology that underlies the ceremonial law is the same theology that Christ fulfills; the former is that theology in shadow, but Christ is that theology in substance. The Belgic Confession spells this out:

> We believe that the ceremonies and symbols of the law have ceased with the coming of Christ, and that all shadows have been fulfilled, so that the use of them ought to be abolished among Christians, Yet their truth and substance remain for us in Jesus Christ, in whom they have been fulfilled.

The fourth hermeneutical principle is the affirmation of the New Testament that the Old Testament moral laws have been confirmed by Christ and His Apostles as being binding for today (Matt. 5:17ff; 22:36-40; Rom. 8:1-4; 13:8-10; 1 Cor. 7:19). The New Testament fully confirms the continuing authority of the moral law revealed in the Old Testament Scriptures (2 Tim. 3:16-17).[27] The Apostles speak of Christ offering a better sacrifice and instituting a better priesthood, but they never speak of Christ instituting better moral standards.[28] The New Testament deepens our understanding of God's moral law, but it does not give us a new moral law.[29] The New Testament completes the revelation of God to man and, therefore, it completes the revelation of God's moral law.

---

laws which built a wall of separation between the Jews and Gentiles have been taken away, but the New Testament principle of separation from the world is illustrated in these laws (cf. 2 Cor. 6:14-18).

27. See pp.29-30 for further discussion of this principle.

28. Greg Bahnsen, *By This Standard* (Tyler, Tx.: Institute for Christian Economics, 1985), pp. 313-315.

29. In the Sermon on the Mount Jesus is not giving a new interpretation of the law, giving the law a deeper meaning, or establishing moral standards that are higher than the Old Testament law revealed. Rather, Jesus is seeking to clear away the scribal misinterpretations of the law and to restore the true understanding of the ethical standards that were originally revealed through Moses.

But one searches the New Testament in vain to find even one verse that disparages any of the Old Testament moral standards. The New Testament exhibits a perfect harmony between the ethical standards revealed by Moses and the Prophets and those revealed by Jesus and the Apostles. Therefore, the New Testament Scripture instructs us to regard the Old Testament moral laws as still binding, and to consider the ceremonial laws as being abrogated. A failure to recognize this teaching will open the door to the abuse of the Old Testament law in the New Testament church.

The final principle for the interpretation of biblical law that will be noted in this presentation is the need to take into account the cultural differences between biblical times and our own day. If we are to properly apply the eternal principles of God's law to the modern world, the cultural discontinuities must be understood and bridged. The task in this regards is to discern and separate the abiding standard of the moral law from its Old Testament or New Testament cultural expression,[30] and then apply that abiding standard to our culture and setting. As stated previously, many of the biblical commands are given in terms of universal moral standards.[31] The problem for us when dealing with these laws is not interpretation or application; our problem is obedience! The biblical commands that state the moral law in terms of the biblical culture will require us to determine the moral

---

30.Some have complained that Old Testament law is too far removed from modern culture to be of any use today. However, there is also a great gap between our culture and the culture of the New Testament era. To reject Old Testament law on the basis of cultural discontinuity would logically require us to reject the New Testament commands as well.

31.For example: "Ye shall not steal, neither deal falsely, neither lie to another" (Lev. 19:11); "Thou shalt not raise a false report: put not thine hand with the wicked to be an unrighteous witness" (Ex. 23:1).

principle that underlies the command.[32] It is the moral law that informs the command that is binding, and not necessarily the cultural expression of that law. The cultural dimension of biblical interpretation is challenging, yet very necessary. However, we must beware that the element of culture is not used by the enemies of God's law to cancel out the teaching and authority of God's holy Word.[33]

The theonomic approach to Christian ethics requires the diligent and careful study of God's law. Theonomists fully recognize that the interpretation and application of biblical law is hard and difficult work, and they reject any simplistic approach to the issue. If Christians are to know and understand God's law, and properly apply it to every sphere of life, they must heed the command of God to meditate in the law of the Lord day and night.

---

32. For example: "No man shall take the nether or the upper millstone to pledge: for he takes a man's life to pledge" (Deut. 24:6); "Thou shalt not see thy brother's ox or his sheep go astray, and hide thyself from them: thou shalt in any case bring them again unto thy brother" (Deut. 22:1).

33. So-called Christian feminists have sought to nullify the biblical teaching on the roles of men and women by saying that this teaching was simply a reflection of the culture of the day and is no longer binding for us. Thus, they use their own cultural tradition to set aside the law of God.

CHAPTER 9 - THEONOMY AND CIVIL LAW

One of the most important distinctives of theonomy is its view on civil law and the civil magistrate. Theonomy teaches that God's law as revealed in Scripture sets the moral standard for all of life, *including the social and political.* Theonomy contends that the law of God ought to form the basis for all civil law, and that the civil magistrate is a servant of God who is responsible to uphold all aspects of the moral law that directly relate to the social order, public morality, and civil justice. Autonomy in socio-political ethics is just as offensive to God as autonomy in personal ethics. The discussion that follows will present some of the basic features of the theonomic approach to civil law.

God, who is King over all the earth (Ps. 47:2, 7-8), has established three separate institutions for our good and for the ordering of human society. These institutions are: the family (Gen. 2:24; Col. 3:18-21), the church (Gen. 12:1-3; Eph.1:22-23; 2:19-22), and the state (Gen. 9:5; Rom. 13:1-7). Each has been granted authority from God for the carrying out of their respective commissions. Now, when God gives authority to men, *He always gives clear instructions on the purpose, limits, and use of that authority.* The Word of God reveals these necessary instructions (*torah*, or laws) so that the family, the church, and the state will be thoroughly equipped for every good work (2 Tim. 3:16-17). This all seems reasonably clear. Yet, many Christians who believe that Scripture ought to establish the laws of conduct for the family and church, reject out of hand the teaching of theonomy that the state is also bound to adhere to biblical law as the standard for all its activities and legislation. Theonomists avoid such a *glaring inconsistency* and properly maintain that each institution established by God is bound to the authority of the law of God revealed in Scripture.

The theonomic view on civil law is centered on the biblical teaching concerning the state and the civil magistrate:

> God, the supreme Lord and King of all the world, hath ordained civil magistrates to be under him, over the people, for his own glory and the public good; and to this end hath armed them with the power of the sword, for the defence and encouragement of them that do good, and for the punishment of evil doers.[34]

The Bible distinctly teaches that the civil magistrate receives his authority from God and that he is to function as God's minister (servant). That this is the case is seen by direct scriptural statements (Rom. 13:4, 6; Isa. 43:28); by the fact that God is the one who places him into authority (Dan. 4:25, 32, 34-37; Jn. 19:11; Rom. 13:1; 1 Pe. 2:14); by the fact that all those who rule over men are commanded to rule in the fear of God (2 Sam. 23:3; 2 Chron. 19:6-7); by the fact that all the kings and judges of the earth are commanded to serve the Lord and pay homage to His Son (Ps. 2:10-12); and by the fact that Jesus Christ, the risen and ascended Lord, is now King of kings and Lord of lords with sovereign authority over all the nations (Ps. 2:1-12; 110:1-7; Phil. 2:9-11; Rev. 1:5; 17:14; 19:16).

Furthermore, the Bible leaves no doubt concerning the purpose of the state and the function of the civil magistrate. The state is appointed by God to execute His wrath upon evil doers, and to praise and defend those who walk in righteousness (Rom. 13:1-6; Prov. 17:5). This means that the state has been commis-

---

34. This confessional summary of the biblical teaching on the state and the civil magistrate is contained in the Westminster Confession, the London Baptist Confession of 1689, and the Savoy Declaration (1658).

sioned by God to administer *justice* in society (Deut. 1:16-17; 16:18). To the state belongs the power of distributive justice which consists in giving to every man that judgment and equity, protection or punishment that the law requires. Therefore, it is evident that the civil magistrate is appointed to enforce the law. But *whose law* is the magistrate to enact and enforce upon those under his jurisdiction?[35] Is not the *biblical* answer to this question clear? If the magistrate is God's servant appointed to carry out God's vengeance on evil doers, then it must be *God's law* that the magistrate is to administer and enforce![36]

The civil magistrate is required to know the law of God and always keep the Scripture before him so that he will rule in the fear of God and judge according to the righteous standard of God's law (Deut. 17:18-20; 2 Chron. 19:6-7). No other standard is acceptable! It is through the wisdom revealed in God's Word that the ruler and judge are enabled to "decree justice" (Prov. 8:15-17). But when the magistrate forgets the law of God, judgment is perverted (Prov. 31:4-5). The magistrate is called to emulate God's righteous throne by ruling according to God's righteous law (Ps. 47:8; 97:2; Prov. 16:12; 20:8; 25:5). The Scripture praises the ruler who upholds God's law and properly protects the righteous and punishes the wicked (Prov. 21:3; 29:2, 4, 14), but "he that justifieth the wicked, and he that condemneth the just, even they both are an abomination to the Lord" (Prov.

---

35. Please note that the question is not whether there will be law in the state. But the issue is: whose law or which law; God's law or man's law?

36. There is a popular phrase today which says, "you cannot legislate morality." This statement is true or false depending on what one means by it. It is true that you cannot make a person or society righteous by merely enacting certain laws. However, it is false to think that civil law can be ethically neutral. Every law legislates morality in the sense that it prescribes certain conduct or permits certain conduct. The question then is: whose morality will be legislated? Will it be God's righteous standards, as revealed in His law, or will it be the standards of rebellious autonomous man? For example, there can be no neutral laws on the issue of abortion. A nation's abortion laws will either legislate life or death for the unborn; either protect innocent blood or condemn it.

17:15). The Bible condemns "the throne of iniquity" as a civil administration "which frames mischief by a law" because such laws assail the righteous and condemn innocent blood (Ps. 94:20-21). The Lord says, "Woe unto them that decree unrighteous decrees, and that write grievousness which they have prescribed" (Isa. 10:1), and "Woe unto them...which justify the wicked for reward, and take away the righteousness of the righteous from him" (Isa. 5:22-23). Thus it is evident, there can be *no neutrality* in civil law. A magistrate will either forsake God's law and praise the wicked, or he will keep God's law and contend with them (Prov. 28:4). A civil administration will either rule according to God's law (theonomy) and be a "throne of righteousness," or it will reject God's law and rule according to man's law (autonomy) and be a "throne of iniquity."

Having commissioned civil government to rule according to His law and establish justice in the land, the Lord arms the state with the power of the sword (Gen. 9:5-6; Rom. 13:3-4). The power of the sword is the authority to inflict punishment on those who break the law. It is this power to enforce the law by means of punishment which is a terror to the wicked and thus a restraining force upon evil in society (Deut. 19:20; 21:21; Prov. 21:11; Ecc. 8:11). God grants the state the right to require the payment of damages or restitution (Ex. 21:18-19, 22; 22:1, 8-9), to inflict corporal punishment (Deut. 25:1-3, 12; Prov. 19:29; 20:30; 26:3), and to execute those who are worthy of death (Ex. 21:12-17; Deut. 19:12-13, 16-21).[37]

Now the obvious and pertinent question is this: when should the state use this power of the sword? What actions of men ought the state to punish, and how ought these actions (crimes) be punished? These are the central questions of penology. Every system of ethics must definitively address these issues. *By*

---

37. It is important to note that the law of God does not specify imprisonment as a form of punishment for criminals. This has serious implication for a nation that has made incarceration its primary form of punishment.

what standard shall the state define crime and the just punishment for particular crimes? Does the state have autonomy to determine these questions for itself? The Scripture emphatically answers, no! The Lord God who gave the state the power of the sword has also given specific revelation in the Bible on how and when the state ought to use that power. Where in the Bible did He reveal these things? He did so in the civil law codes of Israel. In the civil statutes and case laws of the Old Testament, God reveals the demands of the moral law in terms of civil justice. Through the Old Testament law the civil magistrate will be instructed as to what sin[38] (evil) he ought to punish, and how he ought to punish it.

The law of God revealed through Moses and the Prophets sets forth the standards of crime and punishment that all nations ought to follow (Deut. 4:6; Ps. 2:10-12; Prov. 8:15; 28:4). By discerning the "general equity"[39] revealed in Israel's civil law, the state will be instructed in how to frame its own laws in accord with the moral law of God. To reject the Old Testament laws which deal with civil justice is to leave the state with no objective written standard for carrying out its mandate from God. Would God grant the state the awesome power of the sword, and then fail to give the state specific instructions on how and when to use that sword? If you reject Old Testament civil law as the standard, then your answer *must* be yes.[40]

---

38. All crimes are sins, but not all sins are crimes punishable by the state.

39. "General equity" refers to the universal, trans-cultural principles of justice that form the basis for Old Testament civil law. Bahnsen defines "general equity" as "(an expression used by Reformed or Puritan theologians to denote) the underlying substance, principle, or point of a law—over against the specific case or cultural setting mentioned by it." *By This Standard*, p. 355.

40. The New Testament reveals very little on the specifics of civil law and civil justice. But of course, it does not need to, for God has already addressed these issues in the Old Testament!

The disturbing fact is that many Christians deny that God intends the nations to be bound to the principles of justice revealed in Israel's civil law. These Christians would rather substitute the standard of natural law for the standard of God's written law. This may appear to many to be the most acceptable standard for the nations, but the rejection of biblical law for natural law raises a number of important questions which the proponents of natural law need to answer.

First of all, where in the Bible does it expressly teach, or even imply, that civil government is *only* accountable to natural law and not accountable to the righteous standards of biblical law? If God has been pleased to bring the revelation of His holy Word to a nation, will He not also hold that nation accountable to rule according to the standards of justice that He makes known in that Word? Secondly, since natural law and biblical law are really the revelation of the same moral law through different channels, why choose the inadequate channel of natural law[41] over the perfect and infallible revelation of Scripture? Why choose natural law which reveals no specifics on the nature of civil government, or the use and limits of state power, over the Word of God which does give these specifics?[42] Some may respond by saying that we live in a secular society that does not accept the authority or the ethical standards of biblical law. However, if natural law and biblical law are the revelation of the same moral law, how will the ethical standards of natural law be any easier for the unbeliever to accept than the ethical standards of the Bible?[43] If there is no hope that a pluralistic society will

---

41. See pp. 20-24 for the discussion on the limitations and inadequacies of natural law as the basis of ethics.

42. By discounting God's written revelation of the moral law, natural law advocates wrongly contend that Gentile nations of today are only responsible to the same dim standard that pagan nations were responsible to during "the times of this ignorance" (Acts 17:30).

43. Unless, of course, natural law advocates really believe that there is a double standard for socio-political ethics: a lower standard revealed to the

ever accept the standard of biblical law, what basis is there to hope that such a humanistic culture will ever come to a true and common understanding on what constitutes natural law? Thirdly, why should Christians surrender the "sword" of the Word of God for the elusive concept of natural law in our battle to establish righteousness in our nation? What possible advantage is there in laying aside the quick and powerful Word of the living God as we seek to call this nation to repentance and to its duty "to serve the Lord with fear...and kiss the Son" (Ps. 2:10-12)? Fourthly, what standard of social and political ethics should a Christian magistrate use to guide him in the decisions and judgments that he must make as God's minister, biblical law or natural law? Is the Christian magistrate to use the Bible for his own personal ethics and family ethics, but then set the Bible aside when he comes to his office of civil magistrate? Christians who propose natural law as the rule for social and political ethics need to supply *biblical* answers to the above questions.

Christian natural law advocates also need to provide a *biblical* refutation of Symington's insightful words:

> It is the duty of nations, as the subjects of Christ, to take his law as their rule. They are apt to think it enough that they take, as their standard of legislation and administration, human reason, natural conscience, public opinion, or political expediency. None of these, however, nor indeed all of them together, can supply a sufficient guide in affairs of state. Of course, heathen nations, who are not in possession of the revealed will of God, must be regulated by the law of nature: but this is no good reason why those who have a revelation of the divine will should be restricted

---

nations by natural law, and a higher one revealed to Israel in Scripture. Such a double standard would also imply that the nations living in the New Testament age of fulfillment and the completed canon of Scripture are under a lower standard of socio-political ethics than Old Testament Israel since natural law proponents believe that Gentile nations are still bound to only natural law and not to biblical law.

to the use of a more imperfect rule. It is absurd to contend that, because civil society is founded in nature, men are to be guided, in directing its affairs and consulting its interests, solely by the light of nature...The truth is, that revelation is given to man to supply the imperfections of nature; and to restrict ourselves to the latter, and renounce the former, in any case in which it is competent to guide us, is at once to condemn God's gift and to defeat the end for which it was given. We contend, then, that the Bible is to be our rule, not only in matters of a purely religious nature, in matters connected with conscience and the worship of God, but in matters of a civil and political nature. To say that in such matters we have nothing to do with the Bible, is to maintain what is manifestly untenable. To require nations, who possess the sacred volume, to confine themselves, in their political affairs, to the dim light of nature, is not more absurd than it would be to require men, when the sun is in the heavens, to shut out its full blaze and go about their ordinary duties by the feeble rays of a taper. Indeed, if nations are moral subjects, they are bound to regulate their conduct by whatever laws their moral Governor has been pleased to give them; and as they are the subjects of the Mediator, they must be under the law of the Mediator contained in the Scriptures. He has not placed his moral subjects in ignorance of his will, nor left them to search for it amid the obscurities and imperfections of a law which sin has effaced and well nigh obliterated. In the Holy Scriptures of truth, he has given them a fairer and more complete exhibition of the principles of immutable and eternal justice, than that which is to be found in the law of nature.[44]

Theonomy rejects the claim that natural law ought to be the standard, and teaches that the nations are bound to the universal and unchanging principles of justice revealed in Israel's civil law. The Old Testament law is a model of justice for every sphere of life, including the civil sphere (Deut. 4:6-8). There-

---

44. William Symington, *Messiah the Prince* (Edmonton: Still Waters Revival Books, 1990, reprint of 1884 ed.), pp. 234-235.

fore, the penology revealed in the civil law of Israel ought to be the rule for civil law today. The punishments prescribed in the perfect law of the Lord (Ps. 19:7) establish perfect justice. The New Testament itself declares that all the penalties appointed for the violation of the civil law of Israel were "a just recompense of reward" (Heb. 2:2). The Lord did not violate the *lex talionis* principle of justice ("an eye for an eye," cf. Ex 21:24-25; Deut. 19:21),[45] which He had commanded judges to follow, when He established the penal sanctions of Israel's civil law. The penalties were neither too harsh, nor too lenient. In God's law the punishment always fits the crime.[46]

Not only does the law of God establish the duties and functions of civil magistrates, it also sets forth the necessary qualifications for those who will bear rule in the civil sphere: "Moreover thou shalt provide out of all the people able men, such as fear God, men of truth, hating coveteousness; and place such over them, to be rulers of thousands, rulers of hundreds, rulers of fifties, and rulers of tens" (Ex. 18:21). If a nation is to know the blessing of righteousness and justice under God's law, its rulers must be men who fear God and openly serve Him as His ministers (2 Sam. 23:3; Rom. 13:1-6), submitting to His law in all their duties and decisions. To seek to establish righteous

---

45.*Lex talionis*, or the law of retaliation, was a legal formula for judges, and not a sanction for personal revenge (Matt. 5:38-42). This legal prescription taught judges that the punishment must be commensurate with the nature of the crime. It imposed strict limits on the punishment which could be meted out.

46.This would include the capital crimes of the Old Testament civil law. Some would argue that the death penalty for adultery, rape, or kidnaping were appropriate for Israel, but not for the United States. But why would it be just for the civil magistrate in Israel to execute such malefactors, and yet be unjust for the civil magistrate in our country to do the same? Who dare say that death is too strong a punishment for these crimes, when God Himself established this penalty in His revealed law? Are we wiser than God? Do we know a better and more just penalty than the one God has prescribed? And by what standard do we establish this supposedly more just punishment?

laws without taking into account the spiritual condition of the men who enact and enforce the laws is an exercise in futility. There is perfect harmony, however, in the law of the Lord: it insists on righteous laws *and* righteous men. So then, just as we have no right to autonomy in the making of our civil laws, so likewise, we have not right to autonomy in the choosing of our civil leaders. God's law requires that we only choose men who are wise and able, who know the Scriptures, and who fear God and pay homage to Jesus Christ, publicly confessing Him as King of kings and Lord of Lords (Ex. 18:21; Deut. 1:13; 17:15; Ps. 2:10-12; Rev. 1:5; 19:16).

Theonomy also affirms that true civil liberty can only be known in a nation where God's law is the standard for civil law. This is because true liberty in God's world is not freedom to do what one pleases (autonomy), but it is freedom to do what is right and good (theonomy). The law of God sets forth the path of righteousness; hence it is the perfect law of liberty (Jas. 1:25). The psalmist said, "I will walk at liberty: for I seek thy precepts" (Ps. 119:45). The law is God's truth, and it is the truth that sets us free (Ps. 119:142; Jn. 8:31-32). Humanistic law, which is based on the lie, promotes wickedness, and this is the path of bondage and death (Jn. 8:34; Prov. 14:12).

Additionally, the law of God promotes civil liberty by defining the limits of state power. The state may not control or legislate where it has no scriptural warrant.[47] The magistrate must stay within the bounds of his legitimate authority. The individual, the family, and the church are to be free from unlawful state oppression so that they may fulfill their responsibilities from God. Likewise, the law of God gives the citizens a standard whereby they may judge the actions of the state. If the

---

47. The state, for example, has no authority to control education or the economy, nor to redistribute the wealth of its citizens according to some scheme of "economic justice" or social welfare.

state oversteps its bounds, the citizens are justified in resisting the tyranny of the state (Acts 4:19; 5:29; Matt. 22:21).[48] Without the measure of God's law, the citizens might never be sure when the state ought to be resisted.

Theonomy also advocates the separation of church and state. The church and state are distinct institutions, each having their own clearly defined ministry from God. The state is a ministry of civil justice by the securing of the rights of its citizens and by the punishing of evil doers (Deut. 19:13; 25:1-2; Rom. 13:1-4; 1 Pe. 2:14). The church is a ministry of grace through the preaching of the Word of God and the administration of the sacraments (Matt. 28:19-21; 26:26-28; 1 Tim. 3:15; 4:13). The state is not to control (govern) the church, nor is the church to control (govern) the state. However, *both* church and state are to function under Christ's authority and law; *both* are to serve God's kingdom by carrying out their respective commissions; *both* are to assist each other and influence each other for good. The state is to shield the church from the wicked, and provide the domestic tranquillity and freedom which will enable the church to carry out its calling without harassment or fear (1 Tim. 2:2; Isa. 49:23).[49] The Reformed Presbyterian Catechism (1949)

---

48. Theonomy does not preach violence or insurrection, but resistance in accordance with God's law. Theonomists would advocate the principle of interposition which is this: when a people are being oppressed and stripped of their rights by a tyrannical government or magistrate, they should not choose the path of individual resistance or rebellion, but should seek out a magistrate or magistrates at an intermediate level of government who will lead them in their resistance. The lesser magistrate or level of government interposes itself between the people and the oppressing higher power. Anarchy is never blessed of God. It is the way of the flesh and the world. All resistance movements should be under a properly appointed magistrate. Furthermore, theonomy would advocate the use of the Imprecatory Psalms as a biblical means of bringing God's judgment on wicked rulers so that they will either repent, or be removed from office and righteous men put in their places (cf. Ps. 7; 35; 58; 59; 69; 83; 109; 137; 139; also cf. Jer. 10:25; 17:18; 18:18-23).

49. The Savoy Declaration (1658), a Reformed Confession which set forth

asserts, "The State serves the interest of the church in that while recognizing the independence of the Church, she exercises her authority to preserve public morals and to honor the true religion."

The church is to teach the state the principles of God's Word by which the state is to govern. The church has the prophetic function of rebuking the state when it departs from the law of God and of calling the civil magistrate back to the paths of righteousness (Isa. 10:1-2; Amos 5:10-12; 2 Sam. 12:1-14; Jer. 1:9-10; Mk. 6:18). The church is to prepare men in both character and knowledge to be effective and godly magistrates. The church is to provide the foundation for a just and free society by evangelizing and discipling the citizens in the Christian faith, and by teaching them to pay their taxes and to give all proper respect and obedience to the civil authorities over them (Rom. 13:1, 7; 1 Pe. 2:13-14, 17; Matt. 22:21).

Theonomy strongly condemns the current secular view of the separation of the church and state which promotes the separation of the state from God and the authority of His law. This secular perversion of the biblical doctrine of the institutional separation of church and state is really an attempt by autono-

---

the "Faith and Order Owned and practised in the Congregational Churches in England," provides us with a useful statement on the relationship of the civil authorities to the church: "Although the Magistrate is bound to incourage, promote, and protect the professor and profession of the Gospel, and to manage and order civil administrations in a due subserviency to the interest of Christ in the world, and to that end to take care that men of corrupt mindes and conversations do not licentiously publish and divulge Blasphemy and Errors in their own nature, subverting the faith, and inevitably destroying the souls of them that receive them: Yet in such differences about the Doctrines of the Gospel, or in ways of the worship of God, as may befall men exercising a good conscience, manifesting it in their conversation, and holding the foundation, not disturbing others in their ways or worship that differ from them; there is no warrant for the Magistrate under the Gospel to abridge them of their liberty." Williston Walker, ed. *The Creeds And Platforms of Congregationalism* (New York: The Pilgrim Press, 1991), p. 393.

mous man to deify the state, and to make the state's word the law of the land in the place of God's Word which ought to be the law of the land (Ps. 2:1-3).

Finally, let it be clearly known that theonomy does not believe in salvation through politics. Theonomy is a doctrine of ethics. It teaches the ethical standards which ought to govern a nation and its civil law. But the theonomist's hope for bringing a nation into conformity to the law of God is not in politics or in politicians, but in Jesus Christ alone! Salvation on a personal and national level is of the Lord (Isa. 33:22). It is only through the sovereign will and power of the triune God that a people can be turned from their sin and become a righteous God-fearing society that honors the Lord Jesus Christ and keeps His law. The evangelization of the lost and the edification of believers are both essential to any true national reformation.

Furthermore, theonomists believe that reformation is needed at all levels, not just in civil government. Theonomy issues a prophetic call to individuals, to the family, to the church, and to the state to repent and recognize Christ as Lord and His law as the supreme rule of ethics. Theonomy seeks to reform politics, but it does not seek a reform through politics. The humanist trusts in the "messianic state" to save him and his society. The theonomist puts his faith in the Messiah.

A DECISION FOR THEONOMY

CHAPTER 10 - THEONOMY AND RESPONSE

The previous chapters have endeavored to provide a basic and non-technical definition and description of theonomic ethics. In this final chapter, you, the reader, are challenged to respond to what has been presented to you in this book by making a decision *for* theonomy. Hopefully, you have already been convinced that theonomy is the system of ethics taught in Scripture. Hopefully, you have seen how that theonomy is simply the consistent extension of *sola Scriptura* into the sphere of ethics. Hopefully, you have been induced to embrace the law of God, as revealed in Scripture, as being the supreme standard for determining the rightness or wrongness of any and all human behavior. If you have been convinced (or if you were before you ever picked up this book) of the truth of theonomy, then this final chapter will serve to solidify your commitment to theonomic ethics and to strengthen your resolve to live according to God's law and encourage others to do the same.

But if you are not yet persuaded that theonomy is the biblical approach to ethics, then it is hoped that this chapter, which presents theonomy from a slightly different perspective than the previous chapters, will assure you of the truth and power of theonomic ethics and cause you to make a decision *for* theonomy. Let each carefully consider the following seven reasons why each Christian and each church ought to heartily embrace theonomy.

Theonomy Glorifies God

Our highest purpose in life is to glorify God. We glorify Him when we think and live in such a way that He is honored above all else and receives the glory due His name. Theonomy glorifies God by exalting Him to His proper place as the sovereign Creator and King of all the earth. Theonomy declares that "the Lord is our judge, the Lord is our lawgiver, the Lord is our king" (Isa. 33:22)! Theonomy is a completely theocentric approach to ethics. It magnifies God's law alone, and totally condemns Satan's lie that men can be their own gods and determine good and evil for themselves (autonomy).

Theonomy glorifies God by recognizing and proclaiming that God's own holy nature is the source of the moral law which binds all men everywhere (1 Pe. 1:14-16). God is the source of all things, including the moral law. Theonomy teaches that all that is righteous, good, and true comes from God (Jas. 1:17). Furthermore, theonomy glorifies God by exalting His Word as the all-sufficient, infallible, and ultimate standard of ethics. Theonomists love to declare that the written law of the Lord is perfect! Every other system of ethics in some way detracts from the glory of God, but theonomy fully glorifies God by exalting His holy nature, His sovereign authority, and His written Word.

Theonomy Sets Forth Man's True Duty

Theonomy focuses on the central scriptural theme that man is responsible to obey God (Ecc. 12:13-14). It unashamedly confronts modern autonomous man with the call to obey God's law, and it warns men of the dire consequences for failing to do so. Theonomy preaches a biblical gospel of repentance from sin and faith in the Lord Jesus Christ, making it clear to all that to follow Jesus Christ means a commitment to strive to walk in complete obedience to the law of God. Theonomy stands in definite opposition to the rampant spirit of antinomianism in the church today. It challenges a worldly and disobedient church to repent, return to the law of God as the standard of holy living, and to preach biblical law from the pulpit. Theonomy is not afraid to confront the modern Christian with the words of the Apostle John, "He that saith, I know him, and keepeth not his commandments, is a liar, and the truth is not in him" (1 Jn. 2:4).

Theonomy allows for *no compromise in ethics.* Its message is straightforward and clear: "Ye shall diligently keep the commandments of the Lord your God, and his testimonies, and his statutes, which he hath commanded thee" (Deut. 6:17). It is not surprising, then, that theonomy has been met with hostility both in the world and in the antinomian church. Nevertheless, theonomists are not deterred by this, for they do not seek to be popular, but to be faithful to the Lord God, trusting that He will honor, in His own time and way, the faithful teaching and preaching of His holy law. Theonomists see in Ezra a godly man, and seek to follow his worthy example: "For Ezra had prepared his heart to seek the law of the Lord, and to do it, and to teach in Israel statutes and judgments" (Ezra 7:10). Theonomy does not get sidetracked on lesser issues, but goes right to the heart of the matter, and teaches that man's true duty is to obey the law of God.

Theonomy Is the True Ethic of Love

Many extol love as the highest virtue, and therefore, make love the guiding principle of ethics. "Do what love demands," we are told. But what does that mean, and how are we to determine what love truly does demand? The autonomous ethic of love fails because it can give not concrete guidance as to what love does require, and leaves each one to decide for themselves. An undefined ethic of "love" is as helpful as an ethical system that merely instructs people to be "good."

Theonomy articulates the true ethic of love because it not only calls men to love God and their neighbor, but also teaches the true conduct of love, that is, the true standard of love. The Lord Jesus taught that the two greatest commandments in the law were the commandments instructing us to love God with all our hearts, and to love our neighbor as ourselves (Matt. 22:37-40). But how do we express our love for God and others? The Bible says that we love God when we keep His commandments (Jn. 14:15; 1 Jn. 5:3; Deut. 10:12-13). Biblical law instructs us on how to love God! The law presents to us the holy nature of God, and educates us on how to worship and serve the Lord in the way that pleases Him. Furthermore, the Word of God states that we love our neighbor when we treat him in the way that the law of God commands us to treat him (Rom. 13:8-10; 1 Cor. 13:3-8; Gal. 5:13-14). True love does not harm another person, but does those things that actually help to meet the needs of the other person. Therefore, the law of God is the standard of love for the law teaches us how to please God, and do good unto our neighbor. An ethic of love that is not rooted in biblical law is an ethic based on a humanistic view of love, which often becomes no more than a cloak for lust. Theonomy is the true ethic of love because it is based on the law of God. As Paul says, "therefore love is the fulfilling of the law" (Rom. 13:10).

Theonomy Is the Proper Response to Grace

The Bible clearly teaches that obedience to God is the only proper response to His grace. God redeems us from the bondage of sin so that we might be His people and zealously serve Him by keeping His commandments (Ex. 19:4-6; 20:1-2; Eph. 2:10; Titus 2:14). Those who have been justified by faith are to present themselves wholly unto God as a thank-offering for His gracious salvation:

> I beseech you therefore, brethren, by the mercies of God, that ye present your bodies a living sacrifice, holy, acceptable unto God, which is your reasonable service. And be not conformed to this world: but be ye transformed by the renewing of your

mind, that ye may prove what is that good, and acceptable, and perfect, will of God. (Rom. 12:1-2)

When Paul calls upon believers to prove the good, acceptable, and perfect will of God, he is exhorting them to live according to the law of God which is good (Rom. 7:12, 16), acceptable (Eph. 5:8-10), and perfect (Ps. 19:7).

Before salvation we were the servants of sin, but now that we are justified by grace, we are to become the servants of righteousness (Rom. 6:16-23; Jn. 8:34-35); that is, we are to serve God and obey His law which is the true rule of righteousness. Paul proclaims the proper response to grace when he says: "For the grace of God that bringeth salvation hath appeared to all men, teaching us that, denying ungodliness and worldly lusts, we should live soberly, righteously, and godly, in this present world" (Titus 2:11-12). Where do we learn how to live soberly, righteously, and godly, but in the law of God? Therefore, it is evident that theonomy is the only proper response to grace.

Theonomy Is the Path of Blessing

God's blessing is promised to the one who keeps God's law. The psalmist says: "Blessed are the undefiled in the way, who walk in the law of the Lord. Blessed are they that keep his testimonies, and that seek him with the whole heart" (Ps. 119:1-2); and, "Blessed is the man that feareth the Lord, that delighteth greatly in his commandments" (Ps. 112:1). The Lord Jesus taught, "blessed are they that hear the word of God, and keep it" (Lk. 11:28). The Apostle John declares, "Blessed are they that do his commandments" (Rev. 22:14; cf. Ps. 1:1-3, 6). In the biblical sense, a "blessing" is a gift of divine grace which brings joy and comfort, prosperity and strength. And as the above texts teach, God's blessing is on the one who walks in the law of the Lord.

The truth that obedience to God's law is attended by God's blessing is based on two factors. First, the law itself is a gift of grace given for our good (Deut. 10:13). The law is a manual for living the "good life" in the world created by God. By keeping the law we walk in harmony with the moral order established by God for His creation. The law instructs those made in God's image on how to take proper dominion over the world created by God (Gen. 1:27-28). Secondly, God is *for* the one who keeps His law, and *against* the one who transgresses it (Deut. 7:9-10; Ex. 20:5-6). God's rich favor is upon His obedient child. God's power and presence are manifested in the life of those who love the Lord and His law. The Lord "knows" the way of the righteous, but the way of the transgressor is hard, ending in destruction and ruin (Ps. 1:6; 37:38; Prov. 13:15).

The blessing of God is also promised to the nation that honors the Lord and abides by His law (Ps. 33:12). Righteousness (i.e., living according to the moral standards of God's law) exalts a nation, but sin (i.e., transgression of God's law) will bring a people to shame and disgrace (Prov. 14:34). If a nation and its leaders will honor Jesus Christ as their Sovereign, and serve Him with godly fear, saying to Him, "Be thou our Ruler, Guardian, Guide, and Stay, Thy Word our law, Thy paths our chosen way," then that nation will be blessed; but if not, the wrath of God will be kindled and that nation will perish (Ps. 2:9-10). As God's blessing rests on the state that follows His law, so His cursing will abide on the state that rejects His statutes (Deut. 28:1-68; Isa. 5:22-24). Scripture says, "The wicked shall be turned into hell, and all the nations that forget God" (Ps. 9:17).

We must understand that the repudiation of the law of God does not only mean the forfeiture of His blessing, it also means the reception of His curse:

> Woe unto them that draw iniquity with cords of vanity, and sin
> as it were with a cart rope...Woe unto them that call evil good,

and good evil; that put darkness for light, and light for darkness; that put bitter for sweet, and sweet for bitter! Woe unto them that are wise in their own eyes, and prudent in their own sight! ...Therefore as the fire devoureth the stubble, and the flame consumeth the chaff, so their root shall be as rottenness, and their blossom shall go up as dust: because they have cast away the law of the Lord of hosts, and despised the word of the Holy One of Israel. (Isa. 5:18, 20-21, 24)

Two paths are set before each man, and each must choose which path he will take: "I call heaven and earth to record this day against you, that I have set before you life and death, blessing and cursing: therefore choose life, that both thou and thy seed may live" (Deut. 30:19). Since theonomy teaches obedience to all the law of God, it is surely the path of blessing.

Theonomy Is the Way of Victory

The Christian as an individual, and the church as the body of Christ, are both at war with the world, the flesh, and the devil. Theonomy contends that if we are to triumph over these enemies, we must seek and keep the law of God (Lev. 26:3-8, 17, 25; Deut. 11:22-25; 28:7, 33, 48-52, 68). Israel's war with the Canaanites to conquer the land and establish the kingdom of God in Canaan is a type of the church's war with the enemies of God to conquer the world and establish the kingdom of Christ in every land. The formula for victory which God revealed to Joshua at the eve of the invasion of Canaan gives the church vital instructions for victory over our enemies today:

Be strong and of a good courage: for unto this people shalt thou divide for an inheritance the land, which I sware unto their fathers to give them. Only be thou strong and very courageous, that thou mayest observe to do according to all the law, which Moses my servant commanded thee: turn not

69

from it to the right hand or to the left, that thou mayest prosper withersoever thou goest. This book of the law shall not depart out of thy mouth; but thou shalt meditate therein day and night, that thou mayest observe to do according to all that is written therein: for then thou shalt make thy way prosperous, and then thou shalt have good success. Have not I commanded thee? Be strong and of a good courage; be not afraid, neither be thou dismayed: for the Lord thy God is with thee withersoever thou goest. (Josh. 1:6-9)

The formula for victory is clear: courage and obedience to all the commands of God!

Furthermore, Paul tells us that we must take up the whole armor of God if we are to triumph over Satan and his followers (Eph. 6:10-18). Now it is very evident that the law of God is part of that armor! The law is truth; the law is righteous; the law is essential to the preaching of the gospel; and the law is the Word of God! Without the law of God our spiritual armor is seriously lacking! No wonder the antinomian church of today is being routed by the world, the flesh, and the devil!

The law of God also makes us wiser than our enemies (Ps. 119:98). Through the law we acquire the wisdom of God which enables us to confound the wisdom of the world, and to pull down all the strongholds of Satan's lie that man is his own god able to determine good and evil for himself (2 Cor. 10:4-5). Obedience to God's law assures us of God's presence as we go out to war (Deut. 1:41-42). Obedience to God's law will cause us to prosper in all that we do (Ps. 1:2-3). Theonomy is without a doubt the way of victory. May the church restore this part of the armor of God, and rise up through the power of Christ to conquer all the enemies of truth and righteousness!

Theonomy Is the Way of Revival and Reformation

There is much talk today about the need for a revival in the church that will lead to a true reformation of all aspects of life. In the discussion on how to bring about such a revival, the primary ingredient mentioned is prayer. Now, it is absolutely certain that prayer is a key to revival, but is prayer enough? A study of the great revivals in the Old Testament is very helpful here. In the Old Testament revivals, prayer was a key factor (Ezra 9:5-15; Neh. 1:4-11). However, it must not be overlooked that every great revival in the Old Testament was closely connected with a return of the people of God to the law of God!

The mighty revival and reformation under Ezra and Nehemiah centered on the restoration of the law of God in Israel. God raised up Ezra to teach the law (Ezra 7:10; Neh. 8:1-8); the people were humbled and led to repentance by the law (Ezra 10:3; Neh. 8:9; 9:1-3); and the people made a covenant with God to keep His law, and they began to walk in obedience to the law (Ezra 10:3; Neh. 8:9ff). Israel's fall had taken place when "they were disobedient, and rebelled against thee, and cast thy law behind their backs" (Neh. 9:26); therefore, God's purpose in the revival was to restore them, and to bring them back to His law (Neh. 9:29). The result of this remarkable working of God in the days of Ezra and Nehemiah was that the people praised God and His law saying: "Thou camest down also upon mount Sinai, and spakest with them from heaven, and gavest them right judgments, and true laws, and good statutes and commandments" (Neh. 9:13). Furthermore, they "entered into a curse, and into an oath, to walk in God's law, which was given by Moses the servant of God, and to observe and do all the commandments of the Lord, and his judgments and his statutes" (Neh. 10:29).

The great revival and reformation under King Josiah began when Hilkiah the High Priest found the book of the law in the temple and had it read to the king. The result of the rediscovery of the righteous standards of God's law was a great repentance by the king and the people, and the whole land was cleansed of wickedness and idolatry (2 Ki. 22:8-23:25). Josiah and the people "made a covenant before the Lord, to walk after the Lord, and to keep his commandments and his testimonies and his statutes with all their heart and their soul, to perform the words of this covenant that were written in this book" (2 Ki. 23:3).

If there is to be a true revival and subsequent reformation in our day, we must pray, repent, and return to the law of God and obey it with all our hearts (2 Chron. 7:14). It is the law of God that will humble us and teach us to walk in holiness. Reformation will only come when the church is led to rediscover the law of God that is currently "lost" and forgotten in our churches. Theonomy is a call to the church to repent, return to God's law, and to keep the law of the Lord with a zealous love for Christ and His Kingdom; accordingly, theonomy is the way of revival and reformation.

CONCLUSION

Theonomy is the view of Christian ethics that teaches that the law of God as revealed in the Old Testament and New Testament is the sole authoritative standard of truth and righteousness, and that Scripture is entirely sufficient to instruct us in righteousness for every realm of life. The Word of God is the only acceptable standard for judging the rightness or wrongness of any and all human behavior. Theonomy teaches that the motive of human action is love for God and man; the standard of human action is the Word of God; and the end or purpose of human action is the glory of God.

Theonomy, as a strictly biblical system of ethics, opposes all forms of ethical autonomy; sees natural law as an insufficient rule of ethics; repudiates all forms of antinomianism and legalism; advocates a careful interpretation and application of the law; and contends that God's law ought to be the standard for the social and political life of every nation. Theonomy, as a strictly biblical formulation of ethics, glorifies God; sets forth man's true duty; is the true ethic of love; is the proper response to grace; is the path of blessing; is the way of victory; and is the way of revival and reformation.

In essence, theonomy is the consistent and faithful application of the Reformation principle of *sola Scriptura* to the subject of ethics.

There may be some differences in some points among those

who adhere to theonomic ethics, but all theonomists would say with the Scottish Confession of Faith that the law of God is "most just, most equal, most holy, and most perfect". The essence of theonomy is a love for God and His law, and a desire to order all of life according to the commandments of God. May God grant each one of us the grace to joyfully declare with the psalmist, "O how love I thy law!"

Let us hear the conclusion of the whole matter: Fear God, and keep his commandments: for this is the whole duty of man. For God shall bring every work into judgment, with every secret thing, whether it be good, or whether it be evil (Ecc. 12:13-14)

SUGGESTED READING LIST FOR FURTHER STUDY OF THEONOMY

Bahnsen, Greg L. *By This Standard: The Authority of God's Law Today.* Tyler, TX: Institute for Christian Economics, 1985.

Bahnsen, Greg L. *No Other Standard: Theonomy and Its Critics.* Tyler, TX: Institute for Christian Economics, 1991.

Bahnsen, Greg L. *Theonomy In Christian Ethics.* Phillipsburg, NJ: Presbyterian and Reformed Publishing Co., 1977.

Bahnsen, Greg L. and Gentry, Kenneth L., Jr. *House Divided: The Break-Up of Dispensational Theology.* Tyler, TX: Institute for Christian Economics, 1989.

Bolton, Samuel. *The True Bounds of Christian Freedom.* Edinburgh: The Banner of Truth Trust, 1964 Reprint of 1645 Edition.

Calvin, John. *Sermons on Deuteronomy.* Trans. by Arthur Golding. Printed by Henry Middleton, 1583. Facsimile Reprint, Edinburgh: The Banner of Truth Trust, 1987.

DeMar, Gary. *Ruler of the Nations.* Fort Worth: Dominion Press, 1987.

Gentry, Kenneth L., Jr. *God's Law in the Modern World.* Phillipsburg, NJ: Presbyterian and Reformed Publishing Co., 1993.

Kevan, Ernest. *Moral Law.* Phillipsburg, NJ: Presbyterian and Reformed Publishing Co., 1991.

Kevan, Ernest. *The Grace of Law: A Study in Puritan Theology.* Ligonier: Soli Deo Gloria Publications, 1993. Reprint of Baker Book House Edition, 1976.

North, Gary, ed. *Theonomy: An Informed Response.* Tyler, TX: Institute for Christian Economics, 1991.

North, Gary, ed. *"Symposium on Puritanism and Law".* Journal of Christian Reconstruction 5 (Winter, 1978-79).

Rushdoony, Rousas John. *The Institutes of Biblical Law.* Phillipsburg, NJ: Presbyterian and Reformed Publishing Co., 1973.

Rushdoony, Rousas John. *The Institutes of Biblical Law Volume II: Law and Society.* Vallecito, CA: Ross House Books, 1986.

Rushdoony, Rousas John. *Law and Liberty.* Vallecito, CA: Ross House Books, 1984.

Simth, Gary Scott, ed. *God and Politics.* Phillipsburg, NJ: Presbyterian and Reformed Publishing Co., 1989.

Strickland, Wayne G., ed. *The Law, The Gospel, and The Modern Christian.* Grand Rapids: Zondervan Publishing House, 1993.

Symington, William. *Messiah the Prince.* Edmonton: Still Waters Revival Books, 1990. Reprint of 1884 Edition.

SCRIPTURE INDEX

OLD TESTAMENT

SCRIPTURE INDEX

ABOUT THE AUTHOR

William O. Einwechter is an ordained minister and the Pastor of Covenant Christian Church which is a member of the Association of Free Reformed Churches. He is a graduate of Washington Bible College (B.A.) and of Capital Bible Seminary (Th.M.) and has been in the Pastoral ministry for thirteen years. He is currently the Vice-President of the National Reform Association and he has had articles published in the *Christian Statesman* and the *Chalcedon Report*. He and his wife, Linda, have eight children and teach all their children at home. He currently resides near Reading, Pennsylvania, and may be contacted at R. R. 1, Box 228A, Birdsboro, PA 19508.